Peter Richards was fifteen years old when the Second World War started and at work as a boy messenger in the Post Office. He experienced the London Blitz, followed by a period of relative calm when the bombing stopped, enrolment in the army at eighteen, and participation in the Battle for Normandy, aged twenty.

For fifty years he was a member of the Communist Party. Now aged eighty-two, he holds a doctorate in international history, and is an active member, as far as his creaking body parts will allow, of the Labour Party.

To Sandra,

With best wishes

Peter Richards.

June 2007.

Bombs, Bullshit and Bullets – In
Roughly that Order

Bombs, Bullshit and Bullets – In Roughly that Order

Peter Richards

ATHENA PRESS
LONDON

ISBN 10-digit 1 84401 863 6

ISBN 13-digit 978 1 84401 863 5

First Published 2007 by
ATHENA PRESS
Queen's House, 2 Holly Road
Twickenham TW1 4EG
United Kingdom

Printed for Athena Press

To the memory of my former army comrades, nearly all in their early twenties, who did not have my luck and never made it to the Allied victory over Nazi Germany.

Acknowledgements

I am grateful to Ms Stephanie Clarke, Archivist at the Imperial War Museum, for her encouraging assessment that my work could be of value to students of the Second World War as well as being of general interest. In addition, numerous friends read the draft chapters that were inflicted upon them and gave me the odd prod to keep writing.

My wife has tolerated my neglect of family life while I sought time and inspiration to tell my tale.

In particular, I owe a special vote of thanks to Nick Jacobs, who gave his time, and buckets of much needed coffee, to read my manuscript and offer important advice regarding its final presentation. Naturally what follows is my responsibility alone.

Contents

The First Few Days of the Conflict

'Young man, do you know that there is a complete blackout this evening?' This piece of information from a well-meaning lady who was sitting next to me during the interval between films in a local cinema came as no surprise. The date was Friday, 1 September, 1939, and I, a lad of fifteen years but already at work as a boy messenger in the Post Office, had gone to the pictures, a popular and comparatively cheap form of entertainment at that time.

Earlier that day, just after the news had broken that Hitler had invaded Poland, I had cycled past London's Euston station where tearful mothers were seeing off their youngsters for evacuation to the countryside. The threatened war that had dangled over Europe for most of the 1930s when I was growing up now seemed inevitable.

I thanked my neighbour for her information but, on my existing amount of pocket money, hard-earned cash could not be wasted on political affairs. So I settled down to watch the comedian, Will Hay and his incompetent partners try to bring law and order to the West Country in the film *Ask a Policeman*.

When I stumbled out of the cinema, I realised just how useful the streetlights had been as people were now bumping into each other and tripping over the kerbs. Had I known that the lights of London were not to be re-lit for some five years, I might well have reversed my footsteps and tottered back into the cinema for a little more comic relief.

As a youngster, I was somewhat used to political crises. During the 1930s, there had been wars in China, Abyssinia and Spain. The Munich crisis had taken place one year previously, and each acquisition by the dictators had been met with threats from the League of Nations, but no action had ensued. A major European war now loomed, even given the threat that modern aircraft could bring about a level of destruction that, it was thought, could herald the end of civilisation.

The next day, most adults seemed to be very anxious. Even Parliament was in session, a most unusual event for a Saturday. So I went to the pictures again to get away from it all. But what did I see? *Q Planes*, a story of secret electronic weapons that could thwart the attempts of enemy bombers to drop their deadly loads. We were soon to realise how far from reality this was.

Everybody who was capable of remembering anything would recall Sunday, 3 September when, at 11 a.m. Prime Minister Neville Chamberlain broadcast to the world that Britain was at war with Germany. Everyone also remembers where he or she was when Chamberlain's fateful words were uttered.

With my ex-school friend John, I had set out for a day's cycle ride in the Hertfordshire countryside. By chance, we had stopped at a little general shop for a penny glass of a popular drink called Tizer and we were in time to hear the declaration. The lady who ran the shop was, I thought, rather elderly. I suppose that she was about fifty. Whatever her age, she obviously had memories of the First World War, which had ended only twenty years previously. Her remark, 'Oh no, not again' stuck in my mind, and later I began to question just why this second conflict had come about. What had happened to the 'war to end war'?

Shortly after we had left the shop, the air raid sirens began their dreadful wail and passing cars seemed to speed up, as if convinced that enemy bombers were on their tail. But it was to be another year before Londoners were to hear the crash of missiles.

As we cycled along, John and I wondered if the War would last long enough for us to be actively involved. Both of us had read such books as *All Quiet on the Western Front* and *Goodbye To All That*, while films had provided ample illustration of the horrors of war, so we had some realistic idea of what was in store. Nevertheless, we thought that we were on the brink of a personal great adventure. This was to prove true, with the award of a Distinguished Flying Cross for John, who successfully completed a tour of bombing operations, and a year in hospital for me after my marginal efforts to liberate France.

The next few days were peculiar. Apart from a few false air raid alarms, nothing seemed to be happening. After a few weeks of closure, places of public entertainment and assembly were reopened. Indeed, all seemed normal except for the blackout. Road accidents mounted enormously, and every evening people cursed and sweated as they undertook the routine of 'putting up the blackout'. But the Billy Cotton Band added some humour to the situation with a song, 'Put That Light Out, Put It Out'.

Oh, Oh, Oh. What a Phoney War?

In addition to the inconvenience of the blackout, many parents wept as Vera Lynn sang 'Goodnight Children Everywhere' and there was a growing number of missing faces as young men began to volunteer or be called up for military service. There were no major battles between the opposing armies and food remained un-rationed and in ample supply. The main shortage was torch batteries, essential to prevent stumbling about in the dark.

It would seem that the events of the period justified the title of phoney war, or did they? Even before the start of the conflict, intelligence and cryptographic services were in action, despite this highly important part of the story only becoming widely known after the War. From day one, the conflict at sea was savage. Merchant ships rapidly became victims of U-boats and in the first two months the battleship *Royal Oak* and the aircraft carrier *Courageous* were sunk. But, in December, the navy had an outstanding victory when the Battle of the River Plate witnessed the German pocket battleship *Graf Spee* being outmanoeuvred and subsequently ignominiously scuttled. The RAF had begun an immediate round of reconnaissance and leafleting missions. Few, if any, bombs were dropped, but numerous aircraft failed to return. It must have been small comfort to the next of kin of those killed or wounded in this period to be told that the War proper had yet to begin.

There were no qualifications to the conflict having begun in earnest in Poland. Not only was the German *blitzkreig* thorough, but the massacre of Polish Jews and other politically unacceptable elements reached indescribable levels of inhumanity. But most of this was either unknown to, or unappreciated by, my contemporaries.

From an early age I had been interested in politics, but my knowledge was only superficial and I found the events of this period most confusing. The German/Soviet pact in August, which had allowed the conflict to begin, and the Russian invasion of eastern Poland the following month, had stood international politics on its head. But more was to come, with the Russian attack upon Finland in November.

The News on the Radio

As soon as the conflict began, the very limited television services in operation ceased and did not resume until 1946. So the radio, or 'wireless' as it was better known, became an indispensable part of the War scenario. Although there was not the modern-day transistor, it seemed that one was always in earshot of a set.

The nine o'clock news became almost compulsory listening, while on the entertainment side the BBC had a field day. The War brought about the transformation of the BBC's Sunday services. These had formerly comprised mainly religious services and chamber music. This cocktail of concentrated misery had sent listeners flocking to Radio Luxembourg in droves, but now such programmes as 'Happidrome' were there for the listening.

The songwriters were not slow to respond to the situation. 'We'll Meet Again' was an early number that continued to cause strong men to weep into their NAAFI canteen tea throughout the War. Other songs reflected the situation. For example, Elsie Carlisle sang 'Nursie', a comic song depicting men who were only marginally ill and seeking some female attention. The song died a quick death when the casualties began to mount.

'Roll out the Barrel' became popular with the troops as they embarked for France, but the song of early significance was 'We're Going to Hang out the Washing on the Siegfried Line'. This song reflected much of the military thinking of the time. Between the wars, Germany and France had built huge fortifications along their borders, the Siegfried and Maginot lines respectively. This, it was thought, would prevent the endless slaughter of trench warfare, which had proven so costly in the 1914 conflict.

An astonishing degree of Allied complacency resulted. It was argued that British reserves of oil and steel were greater than those of Germany. And did we not have an Empire, which would prove invaluable if schemes were to go awry? So all we had to do was sit tight and wait for Germany to run short of vital materials. 'Time,' we were told, 'is on our side.'

Most people believed that the Maginot Line extended along the Franco-Belgian border and reached the coast. After all, had not the German army sought to reach Paris in 1914 by violating Belgian neutrality? Surely the Allied command was aware of this and would not rely on Hitler, who had repeatedly broken his word, not to be such a cad as to invade Belgium? But this part of the story comes later.

Meanwhile, back in London I had resumed most of my peacetime pursuits. The youth club to which I belonged had reopened and sporting activities resumed. One big difference was that going out for a training run became somewhat dangerous, even though the normally ill-lit sections of Regent's Park looked much the same. One strange development was that some of the lounge lizard club members, whose activities had been confined to telling the sporting activists how they should improve their prowess, now, with the prospect of military service before them, decided that they should get themselves fit.

One moonlit evening, a group of such members, guided by the more active types, set out to run to the park. At least two hundred yards had been covered when one of them suddenly stopped. 'I'm tired!' he exclaimed. 'I think I'll have a fag.' From the pockets of his ample shorts he withdrew his desired cigarettes and complementary matches. Had 'Disgusted, Tunbridge Wells' been writing at the time, his disgust could not have matched the scorn I felt for this lack of application.

Gradually, the days grew shorter and the cold became more severe. At Christmas, my family celebrated in the usual way. Nobody was missing, but the atmosphere was subdued. So what would 1940 bring? Little did we know what a horrible year lay before us.

1940: Where Have all the Bluebirds Gone?

Gradually the War began to be felt more acutely by civilians. Early in the new year, food rationing was introduced, and by the summer most consumer products were either rationed or in short supply. My main concern at the time was to obtain supplies of Brylcreem, a hairdressing product particularly popular with young men. Beer went up in price and down in strength, but this was of no concern to me for a little while yet. Smoking became more popular, especially among women, mainly owing to the tension when the bombing began in earnest and the lack of alternatives for leisure spending. But those addicted had to make do with some horrible brands that quickly disappeared in the post-war period.

Although little seemed to be happening at the beginning of the year, there was an air of unease; would all hell be let loose at any moment, or were there secret moves afoot to patch up a peace? The wireless was there to cheer us up and the ever-popular bandleader, Billy Cotton, sang 'Don't Pinch My Ration of Butter'. On a more sober note, Phyllis Robbins, a former singer with Henry Hall's famous orchestra, sang ' 'Til the Lights of London Shine Again', a theme that was to be repeated throughout the conflict.

In March, Finland was finally defeated by the Soviet Union and for a moment the War seemed to change into an even lower gear. Not for long, however, for in April Hitler invaded Denmark and Norway. The British forces counter-attacked in Norway and in the early stages the British Prime Minister claimed that Hitler had 'missed the bus'. Unfortunately, it was the British who had miscalculated and Germany remained in occupation of the two Scandinavian countries until the last days of the War.

Chamberlain's pre-war record of appeasement, and his administration's inept handling of the Norwegian invasion, brought about the downfall of his government. Ironically,

Winston Churchill, then First Lord of the Admiralty, had a major responsibility for the Norwegian disaster, but his pre-war record of opposition to Hitler stood him in good stead for the rapid turn of events that had already started. On the very day that Chamberlain resigned, Friday, 10 May, the German army launched its massive offensive through the Low Countries and the Ardennes. Suddenly, far from being on the winning side, the stark reality arose that we could now easily lose the War.

Hitler had not only violated Dutch and Belgian neutrality, but he had chosen the Whitsun weekend holiday to upset the applecart. How dare he act so arbitrarily! I was furious when the bank holiday was cancelled. This meant that the cycle trip to the Isle of Wight that my friend John and I had planned had received a direct hit from Hitler's Panzers. Large sections of southern England were immediately declared defence areas and cordoned off appropriately. We realised that no slick talking on our part would convince the military that our bike ride was vital to the national interest.

The speed of the German advance was staggering, and each news bulletin grew worse as the Panzers neared Dunkirk. At the end of May, I celebrated my sixteenth birthday, and one week later I tottered out of a Civil Service examination that was to determine my future position in the Post Office. Whether or not there would be any worthwhile future was thrown into doubt by the newspaper headlines regarding the completion of the Dunkirk evacuation and the pending collapse of France. While the news that so many British troops had managed to escape was to be welcomed, the fact remained that Dunkirk was a major retreat and defeat was now staring us in the face.

Dad's Army Falls In

In those terrible summer days when a German invasion loomed large, Churchill rallied the nation with his famous speech, 'We shall fight them on the beaches, we shall never surrender.' To this end, the formation of the Local Defence Volunteers (quickly altered to the Home Guard) was announced. Recruits to this new body were, in the main, either too young or too old for regular military service, and no doubt the post-war success of the aptly-named TV programme, *Dad's Army* was largely due to the fact that its hilarious episodes were not so far divorced from reality. I can well remember those long summer evenings when Captain Mainwarings and Private Pikes, using broomsticks and miscellaneous pieces of wood as make-believe rifles, cavorted around Hampstead Heath. They reminded me, a cynical sixteen year old, of boys playing soldiers.

A ploy to make the population at large feel that it was actively involved in the war effort was the call for the surrender of all aluminium kitchen utensils. These, we were told, would be melted down and used in aircraft manufacture. But, in reality, flying saucepans were confined to domestic disputes. A similar ploy was the compulsory acquisition of garden and park railings, which were declared necessary for making weapons. However, the people who mostly gained from this measure were lovers, who could now enter the parks at night and stay until exhausted.

In the immediate pre-war years, Winston Churchill had been reviled by his own Conservative Party, mainly because of his opposition to Chamberlain's policies of appeasement. Owing to Churchill's anti-trade union stance and his hatred of socialist ideas, he was also disliked intensely by the Labour movement. But suddenly he became a very popular national figure, mainly due to his uncompromising rejection of offers from Germany to end the War and a widespread belief that, if Britain were to stand any chance of winning, he was the man to lead the country. Undoubtedly, any negotiated settlement would have resulted ultimately in complete subjugation, for Hitler's record showed that he would have had no hesitation in reneging on concessions he may have granted Britain in any settlement.

I listened as some adults argued that we could not win the War. They pointed out that, in the 1914–18 conflict, Britain had major allies for most of the duration that included France, Imperial Russia and the United States. Now, in 1940, France had been defeated, Soviet Russia was a near ally of Germany and, in an American election year, President Roosevelt promised that his return to office would see no American entry into the War.

On the other hand, the British navy was still a formidable fighting force, the RAF was more than showing its worth and, although the army had just received a bloody nose, it was by no means knocked out. We still had the Empire and there was no doubt that somehow, somewhere, we would muddle through. Perhaps the scenario would change, perhaps America would, after all, come into the conflict. Perhaps, perhaps?

In June, the Battle of Britain began and, as the war in the air intensified, any interest in cricket scores was superseded by the reported number of aircraft losses. Adding to the thrill of the combat was the undisputed fact that German losses were exceeding those of the British. At this stage, many young men found the idea of zooming through the skies shooting down evil-looking Nazi attackers attractive, and some of my friends, whose main prowess at arithmetic was to 'take the chalk' at dart matches, began to enrol for maths classes with the aim of becoming eligible for aircrew selection. But most young men had no idea of the bowel-gripping fear that many pilots were experiencing as they came near to exhaustion. Churchill was not slow in acknowledging the enormous debt that the country owed to 'the few'.

Such songs as 'If I only Had Wings' and 'He Wants To Be a Pilot, Bless His Heart' appeared and were sung with meaning. However, the number that epitomised the period was Vera Lynn's rendition of 'There'll be Bluebirds over the White Cliffs of Dover', which not only reflected the sadness of the situation, but expressed hope for the future.

The Smell Had to be Seen to be Believed

September proved a vital month, as the Battle of Britain reached its climax with the RAF's daily score at its highest level, despite its reserves almost exhausted. But suddenly there came a change in German tactics. The mass daylight raids ceased, and at about the same time Hitler postponed – and eventually cancelled – 'Operation Sealion', the German plan to invade Britain. These changes, however, did not mean peace for London. Far from it, for during the afternoon of Saturday, 7 September, the aerial devastation of the London docks heralded the beginning of what became known as the Blitz. Germany's defeat of France in June meant that its *Luftwaffe* was now able to sustain air raids against London lasting from dusk until dawn and attack other cities almost at will.

At the start of the Blitz, there were at least three options facing Londoners. They could carry on living as normally as possible and seek refuge in their own homes, take to the numerous public air raid shelters, or 'go down the tube'. Despite government orders that the London Underground stations were not to be used as shelters, the people took the law into their own hands and invaded the stations in large numbers. Whether or not the tubes were safe was open to question, for there were the dangers of flooding and blast. Indeed, a direct hit happened at the Bank underground station, and the death toll was high. In addition, there was the danger of people panicking in their haste to get below and being crushed should somebody slip upon the stairs and a huge pile up of bodies result. This type of incident occurred at Bethnal Green, which was the worst realisation of this possibility. But the fact was that most tube shelterers felt safe, and that was a deciding factor.

The influx of people into every nook and cranny of station space threw an unexpected burden on the ventilation systems. But what undoubtedly added most to the fragrance of the occasion was the absence of toilet facilities. Just how people incarcerated for many hours managed to control their bodily functions is a story that to my knowledge has never been told. Perhaps this is just as well, for it might only offer variations on the theme of an incident I saw when a rather shamefaced man emptied the contents of a chamber pot on to the line. The pressures of wartime life, and the poor washing facilities of the period, resulted in a wide variety of body odours adding to the smell of stale urine. But, after the first few weeks of the Blitz, the Government accepted defeat on its policy regarding the non-use of tubes as shelters, and portable toilets were installed fairly quickly.

However, there were other problems with underground life; especially disputes over space. At times, war below ground seemed about to rival that being waged above. But systems of space allocation helped to restore calm and the introduction of other facilities followed. After a while, it was possible to obtain the all-important cup of tea and, if lucky, a bun as well. In the early part of the evening, singsongs would often be organised and various musical instruments would add to the occasion.

But, sometimes, stability would be upset after the night of a particularly heavy raid. This would induce many who had begun to sleep aloft to return to the tube, and disputes would then occur concerning lapsed space allocations. However, bliss was found by some couples who, under the cover of the blankets, were momentarily unconcerned as to whether they died or not. Shelter liaisons and Civil Defence romances were often the cause of matrimonial break-ups.

Occasionally, shelterers returning after the morning all-clear had sounded found that their homes had been destroyed, or were unable to gain entry to their dwellings because of a nearby unexploded bomb. Units of the Royal Engineers would then either defuse these missiles on the spot, or rush them to open spaces to be exploded. This type of operation was extremely dangerous, as bombs were often booby-trapped and nobody knew when a timing device would expire. On at least one occasion, a lorry carrying a bomb that was dashing to Hackney Marshes blew up as it was passing a crowded bus stop.

Much to my dismay, my Uncle Bill had begun to sleep down the tube. As a boy, I had sat at his feet as he recounted his First World War adventures, which had led me to the conclusion that he had won the conflict single-handed. Now he was proving something of a fallen idol. What a fool I was, and it was not long before I learnt that one has only a limited amount of courage and can only stand so much. Later I was to make mental apologies to my uncle for thinking ill-informed ideas about him. I had not yet experienced the gut-wrenching fears that were to come as situations became ever-more frightening.

Among those who opted to stay above ground were people who took the line, 'If death is at hand, why not meet it in the comfort of one's bed?' However, they had to decide where to put the bed and where the safest place was in one's home. Was it better to sleep in the basement and have the 'protection' of the upper storeys, or was it more sensible to sleep on the top floor and fall with the building, should it receive a hit? It was a delightful choice unless, of course, one never had a basement or the option of a top floor.

Other theories on home safety included sleeping under the stairs, or resorting to an indoor, cage-like 'Morrison' shelter –

providing one did not suffer from claustrophobia. Another choice, if one had a garden or backyard, was to risk catching double pneumonia from sleeping in a waterlogged tin box affair called an 'Anderson' shelter. Was there no end to the variety of ways to make an undignified exit?

The situation was not without its humour. I well remember an elderly man who had scorned the shelters, telling me that a nearby bomb had so shaken his house that it brought down the bugs from the walls and ceiling. In this period, many of the houses in London waged a constant war against vermin, a situation due, no doubt, to the far lower standards of cleanliness that prevailed. 'I don't mind the bombs,' the elderly man told me, 'but when you get bugs raining down on you it's too much.'

The Battle Above Ground

The grim battle above ground to control the situation was being fought by a wide range of personnel, including firefighters, air raid wardens, heavy rescue experts, ambulance drivers and police. Hospital staff carried on and everything possible was done to evacuate patients to safer areas. The bravery of these people was amazing, and the casualty rates high. Newspaper pictures of children being pulled from bombed buildings were very moving.

I recall a conversation with a heavy rescue worker, Joe, who was an elder brother of one of my friends. He told me that, apart from the priority of trying to extricate wounded people from the rubble, the removal of the dead was important for health and morale purposes. On one occasion, Joe had been told that a person was in the rubble somewhere, but where? 'Finally we found him' said Joe. 'The blast had carried him up what remained of the chimney!'

Joe was a mild-mannered man and I have often thought what a shock it must have been for him to experience such a gruesome find. But then I was told of other Civil Defence personnel having to pick up a variety of human remains when a blast had done its deadly work.

I spent most nights of the early Blitz sleeping in the basement of the house where my family lived in Camden Town, which is about two miles from Trafalgar Square, with my brother and my cousin

Nobby. We tried to carry on as normally as possible, going to the cinema, visiting a gym and calling on friends. Nobby had a set of weightlifting apparatus in his home, which was in the neighbourhood. So I made a practice of going to his place several nights a week for a workout, and tried to arrive before the nightly air raid sirens emitted their dreadful wail. Nobby lived with his parents in the top half of a house in Kentish Town and, as his folks usually took to the shelters, we were alone. But not quite, for in the bottom half of the house lived a lady whom we considered to be oversensitive to noise – a most unfortunate condition to be in at that time.

Lifting weights is one thing, putting them down is another – especially if one is working out in the confines of a house. Unlike in a gymnasium, in a house the barbell cannot simply be dropped. With this in mind, we were both very careful and sought to avoid letting the weights fall. But, invariably, mishaps occurred and a weight would make a too-rapid descent to the floor. When this happened, and the usual air raid was taking place, Mrs Downstairs would complain bitterly, saying that she thought that the house had been hit.

Then one evening, when Nobby and I had finished our exertions, a bomb fell on Camden School for Girls that was only some hundred yards away. The noise of the explosion and the fall of the building was enough to wake the dead. It certainly roused Mrs Downstairs, who raced up to us, screaming that she was going to complain to the landlord about our anti-social behaviour in making so much noise. It was only when she saw that the weights had been packed away and we were preparing to leave that she realised that we were not the guilty party.

In the mid-1960s, I attended a parents' evening at the war-torn Camden School for Girls, where my daughter was a pupil. At the meeting, attention was centred upon the reconstruction work that had just been completed and the potential developments envisaged. During the interval for refreshments, I was able to tell all and sundry that I had a vested interest in the reconstruction work, seeing that I had been falsely accused of causing the building's collapse in the first place.

Like most people who ventured on to the streets during an air raid, I quickly learnt certain lessons. If the distinctive low drone of an enemy aircraft was immediately above, then one looked round for a doorway. For if the anti-aircraft guns opened up, one could then shelter from the rain of shrapnel that invariably followed. The noise that the pieces of shrapnel made as they hit roofs and street objects could be frightening. Luckily there were few parked cars in those days, otherwise present-day car vandalism would have appeared small beer.

I well remember one morning, as I left home for work, when I glanced down the adjoining street, which had been cordoned off. There, dangling in a tree, was an aerial landmine. This type of missile was on the same principle as those used at sea; namely, a container of high explosives with detonators on the sides to explode upon impact. An aerial landmine would float down from an enemy aircraft by parachute and, when its detonators struck a building at just above ground level, it would cause the maximum amount of damage. Often, whole blocks of flats would be flattened.

When I saw the mine dangling nearby, I must confess that I gulped something like the cat in the *Tom and Jerry* cartoons when confronted by the ferocious bulldog. But by evening the mine had gone, and one could look forward to another night of routine bombing.

The newspapers of the day carried a wide range of 'sunshine stories' aimed at boosting morale. Bombed-out people, it would seem, laughed and joked as they picked a few of their belongings from the rubble. But these stories became counter-productive when it was realised that such accounts were just propaganda.

For those who have never experienced the delights of an air raid, the Imperial War Museum in London offers a realistic simulated surface shelter experience. As one sits upon the narrow wooden benches, which were a feature of such shelters, the recorded voice of an 'air-raid warden' describes his duties while the sound of falling bombs punctuates his address. Suddenly the shelter is rocked by a 'near miss'. Then, after the 'all clear' siren wails, one is led out to a mock-up of devastated buildings still smouldering. The only absent feature from the scenario is the associated smells.

Bad as all this was, the situation in occupied Europe was much worse. In Poland, for example, deportations, summary executions and near or actual starvation were the order of the day. One year later, the civilian population of the Soviet Union was to suffer unprecedented horrors. But we in Britain knew little of what was happening abroad, nor were we able to envisage the savage development of the conflict.

As the autumn progressed, the intensity of the raids would sometimes wane, either because of weather conditions or German concentration on other ports or cities. Coventry was an extreme example of Nazi wrath when, on 14 November, the city was devastated. These changes in tactics induced many Londoners to vary their activities. Although nearly everybody was tired from long hours of work and interrupted sleep, all sorts of pursuits were followed. Tea dances and lunchtime piano recitals became very popular. Then, as ever, was the all-time favourite; the cinema.

My mother had always been an avid fan of the cinema and some of my earliest memories are of being taken to 'the pictures' when I was too young to read the subtitles of the current silent films. Pleas of, 'What does it say mum?' were met with hisses from nearby cinemagoers.

But where were the safest seats in the wartime cinemas? Should one sit in the back stalls – assuming one could afford such a luxury – and have the 'protection' of the balcony above, or sit nearer to the front and risk only the descent of the roof without the increased weight of the dress circle? To 'bring the house down' had assumed an entirely new meaning.

Austerity had hit the cinemas. No longer did charming young ladies parade in the interval with trays containing chocolates and sweets for sale. Such items were either rationed or completely unobtainable. Ice cream was about to disappear, but just before it did it was possible to buy a small tub – providing it was vanilla flavour. However, the customary wooden spoon was no longer supplied and one was advised to use the lid of the tub as an alternative. As these lids were made of inferior cardboard, they quickly became as soft as the ice cream itself. To try to scoop out the cream with such a floppy utensil in the dark could have disastrous consequences for one's clothing. Regular cinemagoers learnt to carry a teaspoon with them, which obviated the risk of emerging into the open looking like a walking wedding cake.

Many of the films were sheer propaganda. Nearly all the German characters were nasty individuals, usually with heavily scarred faces, and were semi-imbecilic to boot. On the other hand, the typical British actor was a Biggles-like character who, at most, sustained a clean bullet wound to his shoulder. But his devoted sidekick would receive a fatal wound, which just enabled him to blurt out before he died that he realised the girl they both loved could never be his and he hoped that Biggles and she would live happily ever after.

The radio was an indispensable part of life, and a fairly popular programme was *The Brains Trust*. Intellectuals such as Professor Joad and Commander Campbell would pontificate for hours over questions submitted by listeners. One such question was, 'How does a housefly land on a ceiling? Does it do a half-loop or a half-roll?'

To this day I am unsure if this innocuous question was not part of some clever ploy to mislead the Germans. Here was Britain being bombed to blazes and staring defeat in the face, while German monitoring stations were no doubt reporting that some of the best British brains were concerned with the practices of houseflies. But, while this little farce was being enacted, a highly sophisticated decoding 'factory' was getting down to serious work at Bletchley Park. If only the Germans had known that, while some British intellectuals had but a shaky knowledge of houseflies, others were making good progress in unravelling the seemingly indecipherable 'Enigma' variations of the German coding machine. If only we had known as well!

There were some encouraging developments in that grim autumn of 1940. In October, the Italian army attacked Greece and no doubt expected it to collapse. Alas for Mussolini's hopes for glory, the Greeks counter-attacked, cleared Greek territory, and forced the Italians to retreat into Albania.

The other bright piece of news in early December was of British successes against the Italians in North Africa. Unfortunately, both these successes were short-lived, for they were reversed early in 1941 when a German army led by General Rommel swept into the areas concerned.

As Christmas approached, nearly everybody felt depressed. Too many faces were now absent from home and, despite a pause in the air raids, there was too much uncertainty concerning what the future held. The *Daily Express*, which in 1938 had assured its readers that there would be no war that year or next, showed amazing perspicacity when it stated that victory would be impossible by Christmas 1940. But it cheered everybody up by saying that total victory by the next yuletide was possible, if only everybody would rally to the cause.

The pause in the bombing over Christmas was brief. On the evening of Sunday, 29 December, I was in the Paramount cinema in central London with friends. Suddenly, the air raid sirens sounded and we realised that the respite from the bombing was over. Nevertheless, we decided that the spectacle of song and dance that we were enjoying was preferable to the sights outside. How right we were for, when we emerged from the cinema, we first thought we had entered an even greater world of make-believe: the whole sky was lit up as if it were daytime. Then came an unusual sound – that of machine-gun fire.

According to the press the next day, the City of London, which had been set ablaze, had provided enough light for British night fighters to take aim. I am unsure whether it was the light from the fires, or the new secret electronic detectors, that enabled British night fighters to take counteraction. Whatever the answer, the 'all clear' sounded shortly afterwards and, although firefighters continued to battle heroically against the horrific conflagration, most of my contemporaries enjoyed a good night's sleep.

Owing to wartime changes, I was now working in the City of London's main postal depot, and the day after the big fire I spent all morning picking my way over smouldering debris to deliver express letters to businesses, some of which had literally gone up in smoke. Ever hungry at my age, I welcomed the order to go to lunch.

The depot canteen catered for several hundred workers and at lunchtime there were always queues before the counters. Usually it took ten to fifteen minutes to be served. Gradually, the queue I was in shuffled forward and I noticed that the man in front of me was about fifty years of age; semi-elderly in my prejudiced view. At last it was his turn and he asked to be served with lamb chops. The lady who was serving explained that the last portion of chops had just been sold and that he would have to choose some other item from the rather stodgy menu. He then turned to me and, for a moment, I thought the poor man was about to cry.

'No chops!' he cried. 'I've been waiting here a quarter of an hour only to be told that chops are off the menu.' Young as I was, I felt tempted to put my arm around his shoulder and lead him to a quiet spot where he could sob. But this would have meant losing my place in the queue, and I was far too hungry for that.

Almost immediately, I began to reflect on the situation. Here was the City striving to recover from the onslaught of the previous day, the country was in dire danger of defeat, half the population of Europe was being subjected to a reign of unparalleled terror, and then there was this well-fed man complaining bitterly about his restricted choice for lunch. But before my halo of greater understanding began to slip over my ears and choke me, I remembered my reactions the previous Whitsun when Hitler's lightning strike in the Ardennes had ruined my planned weekend cycling trip. Had I matured so much in the intervening months?

And so, 1940 literally burnt itself out. Was it our finest hour or our supreme effort to recover from a series of horrible mistakes? History was about to judge.

1941: And Things Begin to Yo-Yo

During the spring of the new year, the London Blitz became more spasmodic as the Germans directed more of their efforts to other British ports and cities. With the increased hours of daylight and the irregular pattern of the bombing, the return to a more normal lifestyle in London was possible.

Early in January, I had another change of work venue when I was transferred to a postal depot in the north-west district of the capital with the task of delivering telegrams by motorbike. In those days only a minority of the population had telephones, so the telegram was an essential means of quick communication.

I soon realised that my uniformed presence in a street could strike fear, almost terror, in potential recipients who had relatives in the armed forces. During the lighter evenings, in the Kentish Town area of London, it was common practice for housewives to stand at their doorways to have a chat with neighbours. As I drove into the street and they saw me, I could almost hear the silence as their exchanges ceased. Then came the looks of relief and comments of 'thank goodness it's not for me' as I passed them by. Had the situation not been so serious, I could have made some joke about everybody being pleased to see the back of me.

It was not long before the inevitable happened and I had to deliver the news to a woman that her sailor son had been drowned. The poor soul dissolved into hysterics, while another grown-up son, with tears streaming down his face, tried to comfort his distraught mother.

A few months after this incident, I was on a Sunday duty, which covered delivery in the leafy suburban area of Mill Hill. It was a pleasant summer evening and a middle-aged man was pottering in his garden. I brought the news that his son had been killed that afternoon during an air training session. With considerable dignity, he quietly thanked me before going inside the house to inform his wife of their loss. Their evening had suddenly plunged into disaster.

Although these and several other similar events took place over sixty years ago, they are still clear in my memory. I am not a pacifist, but when I hear of war being spoken about as some type of gung-ho episode, my mind turns to the acute anguish of those bereaved relatives. But, of course, not all the news was bad. I remember being able to inform one man that his son, previously reported missing in action, was safe, albeit as a prisoner of war. For one worrying moment, I thought that the delighted man was going to kiss me.

As the year progressed, the Blitz and service in the forces were taking their toll, and news of friends being killed or injured became fairly common. One young female member of my youth club had two boyfriends killed in rapid succession and she felt, and was regarded, as something of a jinx.

In April, I visited a workmate at his home in Edmonton, a cycle ride of about six miles. After an evening spent listening to records, I was about to leave when the sirens sounded; an intense raid was about to begin. It was not a very pleasant ride home. Indeed, as the guns thundered overhead, and several streets became thick with smoke from newly-lit fires, I experienced some of the bowel-gripping fears that were to become periodic visitors before the conflict was over. I felt so vulnerable riding on a bicycle, and a bit of a nuisance as emergency vehicles sped to the scene of 'incidents'.

On reaching home my worries were not yet over, for I had to answer to my mother, who argued that I should have known better than to ride a bicycle through such a raid. I was tempted to say that she was quite right and if only Hitler would inform me of his intentions I should avoid similar excursions. But I made no such comments, as respect for Mum's standing precluded such insolence.

Another concentrated raid took place later in April and for most civilians it was little consolation to know that the RAF was intensifying its bombing of Germany. A propaganda film, *Target for Tonight*, had stressed that our planes, unlike the Germans', were only aiming at military objectives and we were keeping to the rules of war. Only in the post-war period did we learn that, at this stage, the nearest a plane could be sure of getting to its target was about fifty miles. Also, it was not long before British claims to be bombing only military targets were dropped and raids of mass destruction were widely accepted as a means of waging war.

What of the Broad Scene?

It remained difficult to envisage how Germany could be defeated. The war at sea was going badly and earlier British successes in the North African desert were reversed after the arrival of the German Afrika Corps, led by General Rommel. For the next three years the War swung back and forth across the region, until Allied victory was ultimately achieved in North Africa in the early summer of 1943. However, in the spring of 1941 Germany appeared unstoppable as, in a series of lightning strikes, its forces occupied most of the Balkan countries or induced their rulers to throw in their lot with them.

The month of May was to prove quite significant in the history of the War. On the 10th, a most concentrated air attack on London was unleashed. Apart from the horrors of the night, I shall always remember a neighbour ushering a nearby resident, whose wife and daughter had been killed by the bomb that had just shaken our house to its foundations, into the basement where my family was sheltering. The poor man sat with a glazed expression on his face until the bombing eventually eased and he was able to wander out to see what little, if anything, remained of his home.

Once again the City of London had been set on fire, and the raid had coincided with the Thames being at low tide, so that insufficient water was available to fight the flames. It is difficult to see how London could have taken many more of this type of raid, especially if a series had been launched in quick succession. But the War was full of surprises and this raid, although we did not know it at the time, was to prove the last of the London Blitz. From this point onwards, I did not hear another bomb fall for some three years, although London was to suffer a number of raids before the V1 and V2 rockets began to arrive in the summer of 1944.

A few days after the horrors of the 10th it was announced that Rudolf Hess, Deputy German Führer, had parachuted into

Scotland. Why? This was the question that people wanted answered and the reason for his arrival was not long in coming.

Despite one or two items of relief, the news remained mostly bad. The main item of good news was that our troops had liberated Abyssinia. As this was the first country to fall under the grasp of the European dictators, its liberation was particularly welcome. But the bad news was that the Mediterranean island of Crete had been captured by German airborne troops, while Egypt was in very great danger from Rommel. At sea, British naval forces sank the battleship *Bismarck*, but we lost the battleship *Hood*. Nevertheless, Germany could less afford to lose capital ships than ourselves.

This was the background to my progress towards adulthood for, in the epic month of May, I celebrated my seventeenth birthday.

Socialising and Socialism

Until this point in time, my interests at the youth club had been mainly concerned with sports such as running, boxing, and weightlifting. Looking back, I am most grateful to my membership of the club for, among other things, giving me a sense of purpose and respect for other people. But now my interests were beginning to change. On Wednesday and Saturday evenings, the male and female sections of the club combined for socials and dances. Whereas, formerly, my friends and I had poured scorn on the lads who had attended these functions – describing them as 'dancing boys' – our insults suddenly ceased. Girls were no longer the rather strange creatures who let their hair grow long and danced backwards; they had charms hitherto unappreciated. So, attendance at these functions became an enjoyable part of life.

Other attractions beckoned. Alcohol, although always expensive in real terms, was not beyond my means. Hence, trips to the pub, mainly at weekends, were added to the agenda. As most of my friends and I were extremely fit, we could consume quite large amounts of beer and other alcoholic beverages. Although a number of my group had already taken to smoking, for various reasons I never did. But nobody took drugs, possibly for the simple reason that none was available. Such items as LSD, 'smack', and 'speed' were a long way from surfacing, and cocaine was strictly for the rich.

While the youth club catered for most of my weekday activities, what about Sunday when it was closed? I had long ceased to believe in any religion and most Sunday mornings when I was not working were devoted to cross-country running or cycle rides. Runnymede in the summer was a favourite spot, with the river a great attraction in the London *Holidays at Home* programme.

Sunday evenings now centred upon a new dance location: the 'Clarence'. In those days the law prohibited the holding of public dances on a Sunday, so a way round this problem was for a club to be formed and in Kentish Town there was a church hall that was hired out to this type of club. In order to gain immediate membership, one simply signed one's name and was given a number which one quoted as the admission fee of a shilling (5p) was paid. Nobody ever checked whether or not the details given were correct and, when I felt in a particularly devilish mood, I deliberately gave a wrong number; it must have been the sense of adventure within me.

For this princely admission fee, some three hours of dancing were facilitated by a four-piece group comprising piano, saxophone, trumpet and drums. The normal routine was for a waltz to be followed by a foxtrot, and then a quickstep. Occasionally, there would be a tango and a rhumba. Local talent often came to the fore, when somebody would try out his or her vocal chords as people danced to popular numbers.

All of this was fairly commonplace, but what made the Clarence unique was the clientele. The men were a really mixed group, comprising petty villains, 'razor boys', lads from the gym, and those who might be called ordinary. The women were far more orthodox. Some were dolled up to the nines, but the majority seemed mainly to enjoy dancing and the male company, which was increasingly in short supply as the call-up was extended.

At least once a month the dancing would be interrupted by a fight among the rival groups of razor boys. These lads would carry 'cut-throat' razors with large blades, which could be opened to become formidable weapons. This type of razor is rarely seen these days, but many men of the older generations still used them for the legitimate task of shaving.

Often, fighting among the rival groups would be vicious, with blood flowing freely and no holds barred. Sometimes a razor boy would be humiliated by having his necktie cut off just below the knot and the main part of the tie stuffed into the top pocket of his jacket. In all these melées the band would continue playing, but I cannot remember anybody singing through such altercations.

Among the razor groups there seemed to be a rule that they would only fight among themselves. Those who did not carry a razor were fairly safe from those who did and, to my knowledge, no innocent person was attacked. Of course one did not step upon toes, but a type of co-existence prevailed.

Periodically, the police would raid the hall, looking mainly for deserters from the forces. Remarkable scenes often followed, with men seeking an exit via the ladies cloakroom, much to the embarrassment of startled females, whose shrieks would add to the general hubbub.

The gents' loo was part of the scenario of the Clarence. To help save the fittings from being vandalised, the management employed the services of an elderly attendant named Tom, who was oblivious to the pungent smells that prevailed. Each evening Tom would have a stock of bottled beer in the loo, which he would sell for a penny a glass dearer than the saloon bar prices of the pub immediately across the road. But Tom would not sell to anybody without his little ritual of reducing some of the toughest characters in the premises to pleading, 'All right for a drink tonight, Tom?' Tom would then look the applicant up and down as if he were being asked for the moon, before serving up the beverage in a glass that had obviously seen better and cleaner times. The surprising factor was that 'pass outs' were freely available and all one had to do to obtain better fare was to walk about twelve yards to the pub opposite. I am sure that students of sociology could have written PhD theses on the question of why Tom was never short of customers.

I had always been interested in politics and history. As the War progressed and cost more lives, my interest centred on how the victorious Allied powers of 1918 had managed to lose the peace that had been achieved at such a terrible price. Friends drew my attention to Communism. I had been a reader of the *Daily Worker* (the Communist Party's daily paper) until it was banned in January 1941, and many of the plentiful publications of the British Communist Party.

To me it seemed that there were good reasons for anybody attracted to the ideas of socialism to be critical of the British Labour Party. Why had it, like most other European Social Democratic parties, betrayed the Basle decision of 1912 to 'declare war upon war'? Was the Labour Party's role in the General Strike of 1926 nothing more than cowardly? And what of 1931 and the actions of Ramsay MacDonald? Were they nothing short of scandalous? The answers were clear: it was in the Soviet Union where the workers had achieved power, thanks to the leadership of its Communist Party and its realisation that it was necessary to establish the Dictatorship of the Proletariat. Oh, if only things had been that simple.

As a youngster who had left school with no educational quali-fications, my knowledge of a very complex situation was, to say the least, superficial. However, with the energy of youth, I began to espouse the Communist cause. I first joined the Young Communist League, then later the CP itself, and remained an active member for the next fifty years.

My Lovely Russian Rose

On the morning of Sunday, 22 June, I was on duty delivering good news and bad when my path crossed with a colleague. 'Do you know, Richie,' he called, 'the Germans have attacked your mates in Russia?' No, I did not know, but as I finished delivering my batch of telegrams in a somewhat dangerous daze I realised that the War had entered a new phase. That night at the Clarence, conversation centred upon the day's dramatic events, and the general gut reaction was that, now Britain had a major ally, it stood a real chance of being on the winning side.

That same evening, Prime Minister Churchill broadcast Britain's full support for the 'Russians defending their hearths'. This was a policy statement of major importance, for it meant that there was now little danger of the War being switched to a joint

Anglo/German crusade against Communism – the mission that Rudolph Hess had sought to achieve by his uninvited visit.

On that fateful Sunday, the local Communist Party held a hastily convened meeting to consider its policy towards the War, and similar meetings were taking place all over the country. Within days, if not hours, the CP's policy was changed from general hostility to the Government to one of full support for the war effort, with the demand for an immediate opening of a Second Front on mainland Europe. Was not this complete about-face clear proof that the British CP was more interested in the Soviet Union than in the fate of Britain?

And so opened the debate in which all active CP members became embroiled, which still rumbles on today. The facts and the arguments concerning the events have been well-documented and discussed. But new light has been thrown on Soviet wartime policies and actions with the opening of the Moscow archives and the fall of the Communist regime in the early 1990s.[1]

For years, I supported the arguments that justified the CP's change of policy in September 1939 from support for the War to hostility. Likewise, I fully agreed with the change back to one of support. I now share the conclusion that the 1939 change was wrong and did the party's credibility major damage.

But if the CP's policy had changed, so had British political attitudes towards Russia. Full support for 'our gallant Soviet allies' was pledged. Senior government ministers went to Moscow to discuss cooperation, and all types of war material began to be dispatched to the Soviet Union – often at appalling costs to British seamen, who perished in the Arctic seas. Mrs Churchill became a leading figure in a Red Cross campaign of medical aid for Russia, and everybody it would seem had turned, if not red, a distinct shade of pink.

Within a few days, the song 'My Lovely Russian Rose' was being played on the wireless almost from morn till night. At the Clarence, couples waltzed as somebody sang:

---

[1] Atfield and Williams [ed], *1939, The Communist Party and the War*. This contains vital current documents as well as a verbatim report of a discussion held in April 1979 of prominent members of the party, most of whom were active at the outbreak of the conflict.

'I will come and find you, break the chains that bind you when the buds peep through the snow you will surely bloom again, my lovely Russian Rose.'

What was significant about this rather sickly cocktail was the sentiments it expressed. From being all bad, Russia had passed to being all good.

Of course, not everybody could conceal his or her hatred of the Soviet Union. Colonel Moore-Brabazon, Minister of Aircraft Production, stated that Russia and Germany should be left to destroy each other, leaving Britain to step in and dominate Europe. Another negative line was, 'Why send material to Russia when it is clear that the savagely purged Red Army would quickly be defeated and the material fall into German hands?' Indeed, for a limited time it seemed that there was some logic in this argument, for the initial Russian losses were horrific.

As the summer months slipped by, the long-hoped-for Russian counter-offensive failed to materialise. Could it be that the Red Army was awaiting the winter before striking? If so, it was paying an enormous price in men and territory. One wondered whether or not all the harsh criticisms levelled at the Red Army were justified.

In the desert, Rommel was earning a fearsome reputation. Egypt and the then all-important Suez Canal seemed far from safe. The euphoria that had been engendered by Russia's involuntary entry into the War was fast evaporating.

Many eyes were of course upon the United States and expectations that America was about to enter the War were raised when the news came through that Churchill had met President Roosevelt in mid-Atlantic. This meeting and the so-called Atlantic Charter that the two leaders produced were important, but at the time it seemed that nothing concrete had been achieved.

Dialectical Materialism and All That!

Many years after the War, the efforts of the comedian Tony Hancock on TV, trying to read Bertrand Russell's *History of Philosophy*, reminded me of my efforts to read Lenin's *Imperialism*. Unlike Hancock, I did finish the work, but my understanding of

Lenin's arguments was, to say the least, minimal. But, with a dictionary by my side, I did succeed in extending my vocabulary. So when I was invited to join a Marxist study group I jumped at the chance of obtaining a better understanding of the arguments as well as the words.

In this way, I was introduced to a whole range of new ideas concerning history, the forces of change, economics, the nature of the state, and the differences between reformism and revolution. It was not long before I felt that if I did not have the answer to all of life's problems, I did have the solution to those that mattered.

Some sixty years later, with the true character of Stalin having been revealed beyond doubt, any 1941 assessment of the political situation obviously needs drastic revision. Yet, despite the changes, I can still see the force of many of the Marxist arguments. Maybe the dialectics of the situation will lead to mankind having to contend not with the evils of capitalism, but the threat of environmental extinction that globalisation and advanced technology are accelerating.

But enough of theory. The month of November proved more gloomy than its usual fog-bound self. Was there no hope of any event lifting spirits? None was forthcoming, and adding to the depression were the stories of contemporaries who had joined the forces, and their accounts of how in facing the enemy it was necessary to be ready to die with one's boots clean.

Even in wartime December followed November, and in 1941 there was no exception to this rule. But the month brought about such changes to the character of the War as to give young men in the forces the hope that one day they would become ex-service personnel.

Pantomimes and Tragedies

Despite the huge losses that the Soviet Union had sustained, it did not, as with most other mainland European countries, surrender. On the contrary, on Friday, 5 December, with the Germans at the gates of Moscow, the Red Army unleashed a historic counter-offensive. The all-powerful *Wehrmacht* was caught with its pants down; a most unfortunate position to be in during the severe Russian winter.

For weeks, the German army was sent reeling, and the propaganda film, *The Defeat of the Germans near Moscow* was later shown to delighted British audiences. The fact that the hitherto 'invincible' German army could be stopped and forced to retreat was an enormous fillip to morale. But more was to come during that momentous first weekend in December.

On Sunday 7, the 'day of infamy', Japan attacked the American fleet at Pearl Harbour and concurrently began attacks upon British interests in China, Singapore, Burma and other areas. Would India, the jewel in the crown of the British Empire, be safe?

What became clear to most of my contemporaries was how little we knew about the Far East. How was a comparatively small country like Japan able to dominate China? What was Britain's role in relation to the main countries of the region? Most of us knew nothing about these matters and had cared even less. We took comfort from the superficial knowledge that the navy, and such fortified possessions as Singapore, would halt the racially described 'Yellow Peril'. But on Christmas Day Hong Kong surrendered and Singapore was not long in following suit.

But it was not only the British who made mistakes, for on 14 December, Hitler quite unnecessarily declared war upon the United States. Shortly afterwards, President Roosevelt declared that Germany would be the first priority in the struggle against the Axis and Japan's demise would take second billing. From the British point of view, this was of crucial importance. Within days the Allied alliance was forged.

Although I had been working in the Post Office for more than three years, 1941 was the first occasion that I had to attend for duty on both Christmas and Boxing Day. Most of the telegrams that I delivered were belated messages of greeting, but there was very little of festive cheer. Christmas Day is essentially an indoor holiday, but on this occasion the outside atmosphere was particularly subdued. That evening I went to a party, but it never seemed to gel.

My main memories of Boxing Day are of listening to the accounts of Churchill's address to a joint meeting of the American Congress and of the warm reception that he received. The Prime Minister's visit to the States had proved beyond a doubt that Britain had acquired a most powerful ally. We now seemed set to win the War. And yet, and yet?

1942: What a Difference a Year Makes!

The military situation at the beginning of 1942 was, in many ways, worse than that of the opening of the previous year, but there were solid grounds for optimism. Although Japan was making sweeping gains in the Far East, and Germany dominated a great part of Europe, a strong alliance had now been formed against the Axis powers.

Of course, there were serious potential dangers. Would it be possible for the newly formed Alliance to organise its resources before the Axis could inflict irreparable damage and make any victory a pyrrhic one? Could the Alliance overcome the political and military differences that had kept them separated before the conflict? What if the Axis were to develop some of the secret weapons that often featured in wild and not-so-wild speculations? It was not until nearly four years later, and the loss of millions of lives, that the optimism of early 1942 was finally vindicated.

Whatever the estimate of the international situation, life in wartime London at the beginning of the year was grim. Memories of the weather are often flawed, but there can be no doubt that those of intense cold, snow, and burst water pipes are true. Then in addition to the usual post-Christmas blues, there was war weariness and a worsening rationing situation.

However, had we but known it, life in London was idyllic in comparison with that in besieged Leningrad. There, shells, intense cold and famine were the order of the day, with people dropping dead in the street and nobody having sufficient energy to bury them. Some years after the War, I spoke to a Leningrad veteran and asked him what the worse feature of the siege was. 'Hunger,' he replied without hesitation. 'You got used to the bombs and the cold, but gnawing hunger was always with you.' The diet in London may have been pretty stodgy, but nobody dropped dead in the street, nor suffered from malnutrition. Although the War was all around, no bombs were dropping on

London and young men like me could enjoy a social life before the military said, 'Come here, I want you!'

As the spring progressed, the military situation continued to be grim as Japan advanced both by land, sea, and air. Germany recovered after its defeat before Moscow, and was doing very well both in Russia and North Africa.

On the musical front, the entry of America into the fray unleashed a wealth of talent. Much of the output of the bands of Glen Miller and the Dorsey Brothers in the States, and Geraldo and Ambrose in Britain, was a great boost to morale. Radio programmes like *Music While You Work* and *Workers' Playtime* plus a bevy of American broadcasts such as *The Jack Benny Show* were everyday listening. Sentiment was forever present and the song 'That Lovely Weekend', written by Ted Heath before he became a band leader, caused many a service person to romanticise over his or her last forty-eight hour leave.

The cinema proved a major comfort. *Casablanca* showed Humphrey Bogart placing the need to wage war above his desire to woo Ingrid Bergman, whilst the pianist at his gin joint sang 'As Time Goes By'. This song, which had first been published some ten years previously, became a firm favourite for the remainder of the conflict. A 'zany' film called *Hellzapoppin* was released in the spring. Its type of humour defies simple description, but it had everybody laughing and talking about it and was a wonderful piece of escapism.

Making Britain Safer!

The prospect of a German invasion was now looking remote, but there remained the possibility that a collapse of the Soviet Union would revive the threat. So I decided to minimise the danger, and, in April, I volunteered for the Post Office division of the Home Guard.

By this time the Home Guard was a very different force from that of 1940, with the bumbling Captain Mainwarings and stupid boy Private Pikes far less in evidence. Just how the 1940 version of the organisation would have fared against a Panzer unit is luckily a question that was never put to the test, but in 1942 rifles had replaced broomsticks and a formidable assortment of weapons was to be found in unit armouries. I think it fair to say that the Home Guard, despite earlier derision, did very useful work and helped to give many young men a foretaste of military life. One might note that no women were enlisted in the force. Women were, of course, playing a major role in the conflict, but not in the Home Guard. How different from today's scenario, where women help to crew battleships and can be seen in all types of front line activities.

Apart from rifle drill and exercises to defend vital buildings, a task given to the Post Office unit was – hardly surprisingly – to help keep communication open. To this end, I was ordered to attend a course on motorcycle maintenance and map-reading. My efforts at maintenance would have encouraged the enemy considerably. The tyre that I had to remove in a test exercise did not have a puncture before I began, but it did by the time I had got it back in place.

The map-reading exercise was more to my liking, especially when I was ordered to take two days to deliver a 'message' to an office in York. The object of the exercise was to prove that, if all wires were down, communication between London and York was still possible. But I doubt that anybody in authority slept more soundly knowing that Dispatch Rider Richards had broken through.

Shortly after this epic ride, I attended a military training camp where I was introduced to the delights of battle drill. The idea of this drill was for one section of a platoon to fire at the enemy in order to make them keep their heads down so that the other section could charge forward. This was a theory that I was later to see in practice.

On the social front, a matter of concern for young people anxious to impress was that of clothing, which was rationed by a system of coupons. All new items of dress now had to conform to 'utility' standards. For example, men's trousers were made without turn-ups and all jackets had to be single-breasted.

Undoubtedly, fashion-minded young ladies were hit harder than men, and for many years during and after the War a way to a damsel's heart was a gift of fully fashioned stockings. Many girls resorted to painting their legs in order to deceive, but such deceptions were often ruined when painted 'seams' ran awry and veered in a zig-zag fashion. Another give-away was when thoughtless young ladies wore open-toed shoes.

On the war front, in early June the Japanese navy met a decisive setback at the hands of the Americans in the battle for Midway. The exchanges were ferocious and both sides sustained serious losses. But victory was tipped in favour of the US, for Japan suffered losses of aircraft carriers which, unlike America, it could not replace.

During the same month, things went badly in the desert when the besieged stronghold of Tobruk fell to the Germans. But, later in the summer, Rommel was brought to a full stop before Egypt in the first battle of El Alamein. He had, in fact, reached his furthest point of advance.

With all this conflict, it was appropriate for Donald Peers to tell all in song that 'This Is Worth Fighting For'. The Russians obviously thought so, too, for the savage battle for Stalingrad was about to begin.

Open the Second Front *now*!

One of the principal causes of Germany's defeat in the First World War was its need to fight on two main fronts. Therefore, to secure its defeat in the second conflict, it was logical for the Allies to open a new front in the west while the Soviet forces battled in the east. To this end, the British Communist Party was at the forefront in demanding immediate action. It was widely accepted that Russia was involved in a disproportionate share of the fighting and if Stalingrad were to fall, as seemed highly likely in the summer of 1942, then a path to Moscow would be open.

Throughout the summer, huge demonstrations were held throughout Britain demanding an immediate invasion of western Europe. Many people, especially left-wingers, believed that political interests and not military considerations were delaying a major attack. What few of us who participated in such demos realised was the difficulty of landing an army ashore and then sustaining it when heavy counteraction was taken by the enemy.

As the battle for Stalingrad intensified, an event nearer home demonstrated the problems involved in securing a landing in

Europe and had a considerable influence on the invasion plans. On 19 August, a large force of mainly Canadian soldiers attacked the French port of Dieppe, and it proved a costly failure. No Allied tanks got past the beach and, of the six thousand men involved, more than half became either casualties or prisoners. The raid helped to confirm the impossibility of capturing a major port by frontal assault, and the idea that an attack upon less well-guarded open beaches stood a greater chance of success. Plans were then accelerated for an artificial harbour, code-named 'Mulberry', to be used instead of a port, but all of this took time and helped to delay the main invasion.

The day of the Dieppe raid marked an important personal development. For some time I had voiced my opinions at political and trade union meetings, but these were internal gatherings and I knew most of the people present. However, as the situation seemed to worsen, I wanted to stress the need for military action. So, for the first time, I climbed up on a Communist Party 'soapbox' at a corner of the local high street to add my contribution to the demand for a Second Front.

Although I found the experience frightening, I was quite excited by the belief that I was helping to influence people generally. Luckily for me, the small audience that I was able to attract was sympathetic, for nearly everybody was impressed by the Soviet war effort. I climbed down from the platform feeling that I had acquired a new skill, which gave me an incentive to widen my reading and be ready for awkward questions.

By late August, Stalingrad seemed to be ready to fall and possibly the most costly battle of all time was raging. But Stalingrad did not fall, and everybody was surprised when, in November, the Russians sprang a trap and cut off the German forces. The loss of life was horrendous on both sides and one recent estimate gives the number of Russian dead as high as a million. What is more difficult to conceptualise is the suffering that was caused by the intense cold, the lack of medical supplies, and starvation. Some three months later came the surrender of the famous German Sixth Army, whose defeat is widely regarded as the turning point of the War.

No popular songs in English were published to celebrate this victory, but in many cities concerts were organised featuring Russian composers. The feeling of public support for the Red Army increased. 'Tanks for Joe' (Stalin) weeks were organised, and increased vital supplies were ferried to Russia. The membership of the British Communist Party rose to its highest level, about sixty thousand.

Meanwhile, the check to Rommel in July proved more than just one of the swings of fortune in the desert warfare. A new commander of the Eighth Army, General Montgomery (later Field Marshal) had been appointed, whose abilities and personality had a marked influence on British military fortunes. Almost as soon as he took over, he told Churchill that he needed more time and extra supplies before he could guarantee victory over Rommel. Churchill listened and, after a comparatively short delay, the famous second Battle of El Alamein began in the third week of October. From this point onwards, the Germans were in retreat in North Africa and their complete defeat in this theatre was ensured when operation 'Torch' saw American forces landing in Tunisia towards the end of the year.

Meanwhile, the British soldiers in the desert had heard the Germans singing a song to which they put their own words, and 'Lili Marlene' was created. A truly British number of this time was Dame Vera's 'When the Lights Go on Again all over the World'. The film *Holiday Inn* was released in September and I remember meeting friends shortly after they had seen it. One voiced the opinion that the film was not all that good and that the song 'White Christmas' would not prove very popular. For the rest of the War, as each festive season grew nearer, men away from home grew misty-eyed as the Old Groaner, Bing Crosby, warbled through the melody.

Nearly every night, the RAF was in action against Germany and casualties among aircrews began to mount as electronic devices of defence were developed.

Remember, Remember, the fifth of November

Undoubtedly the battles of El Alamein and Stalingrad had pushed the War into a phase that Churchill later described as 'the end of the beginning'. However, in my dreams I like to think that there was another factor which helped: namely, that on 5 November I joined the army. Possibly because of professional jealousy, none of the Allied generals has mentioned this fact in their extensive memoirs.

For the next six weeks, I went through the pleasures of recruits' training, an experience that no person is likely to forget. I quickly learned how to react to such invitations as, 'Come here, you horrible man,' and 'You're a bloody goon – what are you?' which came all too frequently from sergeants and lesser NCOs. The obvious reaction was simple: say nothing and try to look not too intelligent.

I joined the army at a camp called 'The Dale', quickly nicknamed 'The Jail', which was situated just outside Chester. Possibly, the intake of about a hundred men was typical of many. It comprised volunteers, conscripts, ex-public schoolboys earmarked for officer training, ex-grammar school lads designated to become NCOs, and a rag bag ranging from skilled manual workers to what Marx would have described as the *lumpenproletariat*.

The idea of the recruits' training period was to knock this diverse bunch into some sort of military shape. Hence, we had to learn the difference between one end of a rifle and the other; to be able to assemble complicated pieces of personal equipment so that one could move without falling over; to fold blankets in a precise fashion; and, of course, to salute an officer. Unofficial tuition came in the form of extending the range and fluency of swearing, lying convincingly, and 'winning' things that were not rightly one's own.

Of the many films made depicting army life, the post-war production of *Private's Progress*, made without War Office cooperation, is the nearest portrayal of army life that I have seen other than those dealing with battle scenarios. Although the film is a comedy, it debunks the notion that the service 'taught young men discipline', a euphemism for threats of enforced degrading tasks (jankers), or army prison.

Luckily my efforts at sport, work experience, Home Guard membership and political activities had stood me in reasonable stead for what was to come. Some men had never been away from home before, whereas others had never had a home at all. I felt that I was reasonably placed in the midst of the different elements.

On the first day of my joining, an aggressive corporal demanded to know my religion. I replied that I had none. 'Don't be a daft bastard,' I was told, 'everybody has to have a religion. I'll put you down as Church of England.' I thought that my bargaining position was not very strong and that I could haggle later, but it took a good year before I was officially listed as an atheist.

On our third day, although our arms were aching from the inoculations given the day before, we had to learn to salute an officer. Our platoon sergeant, a red-faced regular soldier, demonstrated what one should do if an officer appeared on the right. 'Turn your head to the right and your arm goes up-2-3-then down and face the front.' The spectacle of very serious Sergeant Smith saluting an imaginary officer was nearly too much for me and I had the most difficult job not to laugh out loud. Sergeant Smith, however, was not amused, and he bellowed forth, 'Richards, you're laughing, you can scrub the passage this evening!' This was an order with which I 'forgot' to comply, and I quickly learned that many such threats were part of an act aimed at keeping the sword of Damocles hanging over one's head.

And so on to my first Sunday church parade, which was a first class lesson in whispered blasphemy and concentrated swearing. However, the occasion was somewhat special, for the country was celebrating the victory at El Alamein and church bells rang for the first time since 1940. Just eleven days later, the Red Army counter-attacked at Stalingrad and took the first steps towards cutting off the German Sixth Army.

To enrich recruits' minds as well as develop their bodies, sessions of 'current affairs' were held, where political and economic issues were discussed. On the first of these sessions, the officer in charge fired the opening shot at me. 'You,' he demanded, 'what causes war?' With my introductory lessons in Marxism fresh in my mind I had no hesitation in replying, 'The inherent contradictions of capitalist society, Sir!' It was clear that an articulate reply, whether reasoned or not, was not expected. The lieutenant went red, an inappropriate colour in view of his true blue politics. He asked me to elaborate and I claimed that it was the competition of the industrial countries for markets and colonies that was the root cause of twentieth century conflicts.

Years afterwards I realised how elementary my analysis was, but the officer played right into my hands when he launched a diatribe against the ideas of socialism and the Communist Party in particular. What he had overlooked was that, as the battle for Stalingrad raged, nearly everybody was at least pale pink politically. There was one further factor to this little episode; my opponent was an officer, whereas I was one of the lads. Nevertheless, all the advice that I had received from well-meaning elders before I enlisted, to keep my political tongue between my teeth, had been blown. Henceforth I was known as Red Richards.

Our intake had been divided into three groups and we were encouraged – cajoled – to compete with each other in rifle drill and sport. One Saturday morning a cross-country race was held, which I was able to win. And my prize? I was allowed a pass to spend that evening in Chester, provided, like Cinderella, I was home by midnight, or, to be more precise, by 2359 hours. As I sat in the cinema, I can remember musing that my many years of training had certainly paid off; no, not an Olympic gold, but a whole evening to watch some propaganda rubbish.

A tough-looking character in the intake was a chap called Dicker. 'See this scar,' he would say to anybody interested, 'I got that fighting the fascists.' This made me think he was on the right side politically. But he continued, 'And this one I got fighting the Communists.' My opinion rapidly changed; the man was an obvious reactionary. So it was with some trepidation that I learned I was drawn against Dicker in the boxing match at the end of our initial training. Dicker may have been an excellent street brawler, but his defence in the ring was non-existent and the fight was stopped in the second round. The advantage for me was that my success over a reputed tough guy had won me a degree of respect from my contemporaries.

In mid-December our initial training came to a close and we were allocated to our future units. Somewhat unsurprisingly, nearly all the aptitude tests that we had undergone came to the same conclusion, as we were nearly all earmarked for life in the infantry and most of us were designated to barracks in Hounslow. As we were nearly all Londoners, and Hounslow is on the tube line, the prospect of spending at least some of Christmas at home helped overcome much of the disappointment of not being sent to units of our choice. But Hounslow and the events of 1943 are pertinent to the next part of the story.

As 1942 came to a close, it was easy to make comparisons between the military situation and that of the beginning of the year. Certainly the tide had turned, but it was clear that there was still a long way to go. The Japanese advances had been halted, but they were almost at the gates of India and were straddled across a whole range of islands, as well as being in possession of Malaya, Hong Kong, and Shanghai. At the same time, Germany's extensive conquests of countries had made their liberation a formidable prospect.

Men who had been called up in 1939 had already served some three and a half years; would they ever get home to their families?

1943: A Distinct Change in the Weather

In mid-December 1942, I left Chester Barracks with a severe hangover; recruits' training was finished, and surely things could only get better once the headache had gone? And so, just before Christmas and before darkness descended on that bleak winter's day, I arrived at Hounslow barracks to join what was called a Holding Battalion. We were all raw youngsters, who had never fired a shot in anger and who were about to embark on the next stage to becoming professional killers.

The trouble was that not many of us were keen on becoming killers. Hounslow West underground station was at the end of the Piccadilly tube line and we Londoners were more concerned about getting home than bayoneting anybody to death. It was at this point that I pulled myself up with a jolt. Where was the young man who had called from the rooftops of the need for a Second Front in order to defeat Nazi Germany? Had six weeks of army life brought home some harsh realities and destroyed aspirations? This was a dilemma that faced the majority of British wartime troops. They did not like army life, but saw the need for the Allies to be victorious. However, I return to Hounslow.

Most of my draft received a twenty-four hour pass to cover part of the Christmas break. During other parts of the festive period, we had to box and cox with nipping home and covering the odd duties assigned to us. Parts of the holiday were most enjoyable but, with entering into warm pubs and leaving into the cold night air, I caught the 'flu. So 1943 came in with my being confined to bed in a cheerless army hut with periodic visits from the medical officer and various comrades designated to bring me what food I could manage to eat.

The procedure of reporting sick in the army was enough to make anybody ill. Unless one was dropping, one had to pack belongings into a kit bag in case of being ordered into hospital, and then proceed to the medical centre. In the waiting room, one sat down with others who ranged from being at death's door to those who were seeking some relief from duties. Whatever category, one was treated as a malingerer unless vivid rashes, swellings, or raging temperatures proved otherwise.

In addition to this variety of sufferers, there were those who were 'trying to work their ticket' and exaggerate some complaint until honourable discharge from His Majesty's forces was obtained. Stories abounded of people eating weird concoctions to induce upset stomachs, feigning deafness, or seeking to prove that they had gone round the bend by acting in an erratic fashion. Meanwhile the majority of men soldiered on, cursing both the bullshit and Hitler.

When I returned to duty, the War was still raging on nearly every front, but, generally speaking, the news was getting better every day. The Americans had received their first bitter baptism of fire in Tunisia and, despite several initial setbacks, the general outcome of the combined Allied offensives was that the Germans were about to face total defeat in North Africa. But of greater importance was the fact that the German Sixth Army, which had been cut off at Stalingrad since November, had surrendered.

Although we did not realise it at the time, Stalingrad was a defeat from which the German army never fully recovered. There was still a long way to go, but the grounds for believing that Germany could no longer win the War were becoming more substantial day by day. What we did not know was that the mass murder of Jews, partisans, and others who the Nazis did not like was gathering at a terrible rate. But, back from the wide front, we were gradually getting a clearer idea of what battle was like as we learned to crawl more effectively, throw live hand grenades, and fire off large numbers of bullets. However, as no flak was coming back in return, some of us became elated, believing that all could be swept away if the intensity of the fire were great enough.

In February, I enjoyed my first seven days leave, just as the news of the Casablanca conference was coming through. Now that the Allied leaders were talking of how to finish the War, could the Second Front be far away?

Upon returning from leave, all personnel had to line up for what was known as a Free From Infection (FFI) inspection. The general view of the army was that no man when on leave could resist the attractions of the lowest type of whorehouse and was likely to come back riddled with at least one form of venereal disease. Hence, as the medical officer walked down the line, each man in turn had to drop his trousers while the MO peered at the man's genitals. My sympathies rested with the MO who, after a full breakfast, might have inwardly paraphrased Wordsworth:

> Dull would he be of soul who could pass by a sight so touching in its majesty / These men now doth no garments wear, the beauty of their genitals / silent bare.

The whole process was, of course, a farce. Even my elementary reading of such matters made me aware that the symptoms of gonorrhoea and syphilis take time to appear – if indeed they can be detected by visual inspection – while AIDS in those days was unknown. One must also question why inspections only took place after leave. As we were nearly all going up to town quite frequently, was it sensible to assume that men were leading a celibate life between leave periods? Or were FFI inspections merely an additional humiliation heaped upon the rank and file? Would it not have been more sensible to have held more dental inspections? But, no doubt, the army was less scared of men biting each other than giving each other the pox.

Return from leave was always followed by a round of guard duties. It was clear that in any barracks there had to be a central point of security and information. But why was it necessary for those on guard to have to go to extremes in Blancoing equipment, polishing awkward pieces of brass, and ironing trousers and greatcoats to razor-edge precision? Changing the guard at Buckingham Palace was one thing; to imitate the procedures at Hounslow was not, in my opinion, likely to bring Hitler any closer to his knees.

Whilst great emphasis was placed upon guarding the main gate, there were numerous points of entry to the barracks around the periphery. During the war years, there were no worries of internal terrorist groups taking action and in 1943, as the Germans reeled after Stalingrad, it was highly unlikely that Panzers would come crashing across Hounslow Heath. But appearances had to be maintained and ceremonial guard duties were part of that.

Another example of bullshitting was the barrack room inspection. This usually took place on a Saturday morning, so all of a Friday evening would be spent on scrubbing anything that there was to scrub, cleaning windows, polishing the tops of coal bins, digging up the garden, and whitewashing anything which had previously been whitewashed.

Usually, about once a month, and just to add to the joys of spring, barrack room inspection would be combined with a full kit inspection. Everybody had to lay out his kit, which had to be arranged according to some detailed master plan so that intricately folded blankets on one bed were in line with others; the bottom of boots had to be clean and lined up accordingly; and mess tins from which one had to eat were subjected to so much metal polish that you could taste the damned stuff until about supper time on Wednesday.

Then, at the appointed hour, round would come some senior officer. We looked anxiously to see if he had had too good a time in the mess the night before and what kind of mood he was in. There was nothing to stop him throwing a tantrum and describing an immaculate barrack room as 'filthy', before storming off stating he would be back late that afternoon when he expected things to be better – thus ruining plans for an afternoon out of barracks.

Schemes, Dreams, and Nightmares

It would be unfair to depict army life in this period as one round after another of bullshitting exercises. Some hard work went into toughening men up by means of battle drill, route marches, and harsh exercise. But, of course, battles are not won in barracks; one has to tackle the open countryside. So there began the delights of going out on manoeuvres, or 'schemes' as they were commonly called.

The first of these schemes upon which I embarked was code-named 'Trout'; hardly an inspiring title. As in all such exercises, there were two opposing sides, with white armbanded umpires appointed to decide if one was dead or not. It was fortunate that the month was April and the weather was not too bad. Later I was to take part in schemes in the depth of winter when, if the so-called enemy did not kill us, biting cold weather nearly succeeded.

What we rank and file personnel did not realise was that, apart from introducing us to living in the open, it was necessary for the top brass to acquire skills in logistics. It is not an easy matter to move large numbers of men around whilst providing them with the necessary support services. On this matter, I found the powers sadly lacking, for they could never coordinate the movements of my platoon with the food truck. On one occasion, a promise of a hot meal turned out to be corned beef, hard biscuits and mustard. On the basis that God helps him who helps himself, many farmers were vociferous in their complaints of missing eggs and chickens.

As my luck would have it, I was chosen to go out on a night patrol and capture a 'prisoner.' In order to maintain silence, our lieutenant instructed us to put our spare pair of socks over our boots. Naturally this brilliant idea resulted in the socks being ruined within a few yards of walking. It was fortunate that we were only playing soldiers, for the noise we made in capturing our prisoner was enough to be heard in Berlin.

Then, as we scoured around the Essex countryside, we encountered another delight: rain. As I became steadily soaked, my memory turned to Remarque's First World War story, *All Quiet on the Western Front*, when the hero, Paul, who after enduring the horrific dangers, muck and mud of the trenches, is asked by his mother, when home on leave, whether or not he ever got his feet wet. The incongruity of the question reduces Paul to tears. My own mother would have had similar concerns.

The scheme dragged on, but at long last we all piled into trucks and headed for 'home'; never before had Hounslow Barracks seemed so inviting. So, after I had changed my socks, I reflected upon the situation. We had only been away for some four or five days, nobody had been hurt or killed and, despite the rain, the weather had not been too bad. Yet we felt we had endured a great deal. What would real battle be like?

Sussex in the Spring, tra-la

Later in April, I was designated with some other ten men to go to a field firing range at Singleton, which is a few miles from Chichester in Sussex. The corporal in charge was a reasonable chap and life did not seem too bad. Our role was to be the 'enemy'. As men advanced across open country and approached a white marker, we had to fire on the red marker some twenty yards ahead. Then we had to dive into our pre-arranged holes and hold up a target to receive the return fire. We would then signal how many shots, if any, had hit the target.

When targets were taken down and hits were recorded, the bullet holes would be gummed over with paper after the order 'check, paste up' had been given. This simple order became part of infantry vocabulary for, whenever anybody emitted a loud fart, the cry would be made, 'check, paste up'. But, of course, not all farts are loud and often an obnoxious smell would silently permeate the barrack room. This would lead to a suspected offender being asked, 'Have you farted?' To this, the stock answer was, 'I should hope so, you don't think I smell like this all the time, do you?'

Barrack room discussions, especially after lights-out, were often serious affairs to begin with, and political and religious opinions were fiercely debated. But whatever the first subject for discussion might have been, the debate would almost certainly turn to sex, with somebody making the remark, 'subject normal'. How many of the stories of nocturnal perambulations were true, one cannot say, but in a pre-pill period a heavy discount on claims of conquests was necessary, lest a soaring birth rate and levels of venereal disease should eclipse all news of the War.

Meanwhile, in our temporary near-isolationism on the firing range, the weather was extremely good. As we waited for men to reach the spots to be fired at, we had time to sunbathe and admire the beautiful Sussex countryside. In such an idyllic setting, it was difficult to conceive that terrible battles were raging throughout the world.

From the time I joined the army, I always sent a weekly letter to my parents, but I was usually economical with the truth regarding what I was, or was not, doing. Equally regularly my parents, usually my mother, would reply, but much more truthfully. Then, one dreadful morning, I received an unexpected letter from my mother that simply read, 'Johnny White missing, will write soon. Love, Mum.'

This came as a blow between the eyes, for Johnny, a first cousin, had been my mentor at the youth club, and the outstanding physique which he had developed by weightlifting had made him an icon for my contemporaries. In 1940, he had enlisted in the RAF and become a flight observer with Bomber Command. During 1942, he had a number of narrow escapes while serving with Coastal Command and enjoyed several brief periods of survivors' leave. One evening, he walked unexpectedly into the youth club and was met by Nobby, his younger brother, demanding, 'Hallo, what's this, shot down again?' which raised a great laugh. But, this time, it was no laughing matter.

Possibly the message of 'missing in action' was the most nerve-racking for next of kin to receive, as it caused maximum concern mixed with the hope that all would be well. In the case of my cousin, the consequences were dreadful. His mother, my Aunt Frances, went on hoping well into the post-war period that her son would return from some forsaken spot, but he had, in fact, been killed when shot down over Berlin.

Several years after the War, I met my aunt by chance in the street near to where she lived. She told me that she had intended to go to the local cinema, but after we had exchanged a few words she told me that she had changed her mind and was returning home. Later I learnt that, owing to family likeness, when she had first seen me she had momentarily thought that I was her missing Johnny. She was so upset that she had to return home to recover. When I heard this, my own tears were not far away.

During the War, I had never flown and it was only in the 1960s, when air transport had become cheaper and safer, that I undertook my first flight. Before boarding, I can well remember feeling apprehensive and vulnerable, despite the fact that all the personnel involved were doing their best to prevent any accident. How different for the wartime air crews who were all too aware of potential attacks from an enemy well-equipped with the latest devices to bring them down. What courage was demanded and rendered.

Meanwhile, down on the ground, summer evenings at Singleton were delightful, and often my group would wander through the countryside intending to take pot-shots at any interesting target with the ammunition we had illegally retained. But we never did fire at anything.

However, trouble arose one day when we were bussed off to Chichester to have the weekly bath that army regulations stipulated. As a treat, we were allowed to spend the rest of the evening in town, but when we returned we learned that one of our tents had caught fire. A heroic sergeant major, dashing forth in an attempt to emulate Fireman Sam, had been met with a series of exploding cartridges. His language was nearly as blue as the smoke that explosions usually emit and several days later we returned to Hounslow.

Summer Time and the Living is Easy

The War just had to wait a moment, for in May '43 I came home on my second leave, which fortunately coincided with that of my close former civilian friend, Roly, who was in the navy. One afternoon, after we had spliced the main brace, we decided to go for a row on Regents Park lake. The ducks never forgave us, as they fled to calmer waters while we proved that the combined ops of army and navy could prove invincible as we cavorted around.

Rowing was obviously not our forte, so we decided to go to the men's swimming ponds on Hampstead Heath. We were somewhat surprised to meet a number of men who we had known earlier and who, we thought, would have been in the forces. Most of these characters were bronzed and had physiques that would make Charles Atlas, the famous bodybuilder of the time, look to his muscles. But their stories of weak hearts, flat feet and other sufferings were most convincing, until they plunged into the water and swam to the raft some sixty yards away at Olympic speeds. Clearly they could have given some of my Hounslow colleagues invaluable lessons on how to work one's ticket.

Both Roly and I had the problem of what we were going to say to Nobby, who we were due to meet for the first time since the tragic telegram announced that Johnny, his brother, was missing.

What could I say to a cousin who I had known all of my life that did not sound fatuous, such as 'I am sure he'll turn up somewhere', or that did not twist the knife in an expression of sympathy. We decided we would say nothing; it was a most painful decision, and once again I cursed the men who had caused the War.

I had been a keen reader of Jack London's works for some years, and it was during this leave that I read his epic, *The Iron Heel*. This book, written before the First World War, foresaw the rise of fascism and the brutal suppression of the working class. It had a profound influence upon me, and convinced me that capitalism could not be overthrown by peaceful means. The way in which the hero of the book, Ernest Everhard, conducted himself in political affairs, and his debating techniques, were my role model for many a year.

But all good leave comes to an end, and I had to return to Hounslow, where I celebrated my nineteenth birthday. As a present, I was designated to join a squad of men who were to tour schools and demonstrate to the youngsters just what infantry soldiers carried. It was all a great farce, as each man had to step forward and announce his role in battle drill. On the whole, we never minded the efforts involved, especially as most of the schools were generous with their tea and buns.

If a school had a playing field, the highlight of the visit was the firing of a two-inch smoke mortar bomb. It was at Dulwich College where the groundsman turned a whiter shade of pale when the bomb came perilously close to landing on his carefully nursed cricket table.

There was one important lesson that I learned from the army: never be surprised to be surprised. Suddenly one morning, as I was peacefully firing off shots at the rifle range, I was ordered to pack my kit and become a member of an advance party to prepare for a mass transfer to a service battalion. Could the Second Front be close? The military situation seemed to be changing so quickly that it could be Hounslow one day, Berlin the next. Unfortunately, such optimistic thoughts were almost exactly two years out in their expectations.

Beautiful Amersham

For a few weeks in July 1943, after leaving Hounslow, my unit was billeted in empty houses in the Chingford area of London, where our parade ground was a nearby public sideroad. One morning, as the platoon sergeant was shouting at us during our drill paces, a passing housewife returning from shopping intervened. 'Leave the lads alone!' she bellowed with volume that exceeded the sergeant's level of command. 'The poor boys,' she continued. 'What have they done for you to speak to them like that?' We were, of course, mentally egging the good lady on. But the pantomime ended all too soon, when a passing policeman ushered her away.

Far more serious activities were taking place elsewhere. The war at sea was emerging from a particularly bad phase, caused by the Germans changing their Enigma codes, which resulted in a major disruption to Allied anti-submarine tactics. In July, Allied forces had begun the invasion of Sicily and the collapse of Mussolini's fascist regime was imminent. The RAF was blasting German cities by night, and American Flying Fortresses were pounding objectives by day. The cost in American air crews was particularly heavy, and it was not until 1944 that the long-range fighter aircraft, the Mustang, came into operation and turned the scales on the *Luftwaffe* over the daylight skies of Germany. In the Soviet Union, the Germans were sparing no effort to win the biggest tank conflict of all time, the Battle of Kursk, involving some six thousand tanks. The importance of this battle has been compared to that of Stalingrad, for the Germans suffered another major defeat that set the pattern for their general line of continuous retreat.

Just before arriving at Amersham, there had taken place the famous Dambusters' raid, which was largely boasted as a wonderful achievement. But an after-war assessment deemed that the raid was only a limited success, and at the cost of ninety bombers lost. Apart from the planes, this meant about five hundred aircrew had perished. One can only imagine the grief that this entailed.

But my unit was far more concerned with the break-up of our battalion and our possible posting to far-flung spots. We did not know that most of us were destined for Amersham, a town in Buckinghamshire a little further along the London tube network from Hounslow.

On the eve of the battalion's dissolution, a number of old scores were settled. One NCO, the son of a famous dance band leader, was given a very rough handling. There had been considerable resentment at the number of short leaves he had enjoyed – which had smacked of minor corruption – but his pride prevented him from levying charges against his attackers. And so, in the heart of summer, I arrived at the camp of the 1st Battalion of the Middlesex Regiment, a regiment known as 'the Diehards'. This title had been derived from the Battle of Albuhera, in the Peninsular War of 1808–14, when the colonel of the regiment had exhorted his men to 'die hard' and kill as many Frenchmen as possible before getting shot themselves. It was all most inspiring; the only trouble was that few of us had any idea of what or when the Peninsular War was.

I had often cycled and rambled throughout the county of Buckinghamshire and was of the opinion that it was the loveliest of the home counties. So I was not surprised to find that the battalion's camp, situated at Coleshill, about two miles from the town centre, was in an idyllic spot. But admiring the countryside was, henceforth, to play a secondary role.

The Middlesex Regiment had a long-established record as a machine-gun unit, specialising in the famous First War 303 model made by the Vickers armaments company. By 1943, two additional weapons had been added to the regiment's repertoire: the 4.2 inch mortar, and the twenty millimetre Polsten light anti-aircraft gun. It was to the anti-aircraft group that I was assigned.

So, for the immediate future, aircraft recognition was a main feature in our activities. Many hours were spent looking at the drawings and models of the front and back ends of the wide variety of Allied and enemy aircraft. Indeed, it was quite pleasant to sit around in the open air discussing whether or not the plane on display should be shot down. Then, of course, there was practice at handling the guns themselves, although firing them was to come later – much later.

The importance of the air war was reflected in the songs of the day. One, 'Johnny Zero', told the story of an American schoolboy who always achieved zero marks for his studies but who, on leaving school, achieved fame by shooting down a stream of Japanese Zero fighter planes.

My attention was brought down to earth with a bump when the sergeant said to me, 'Richards, you look reasonably intelligent,' and I awaited being apportioned some dreadful task which such remarks usually heralded. 'You can be the company boiler man.' Henceforth, it was my job to keep the primitive stove that heated the water for washing and showering alight.

I think that I could have kept it alight; the main problem was getting it going in the first place. All over Europe, cities like Hamburg were going up in flames – indeed, the first firestorms were being reported – but back in Amersham my fire-raising efforts only resulted in a thick black smoke that choked everybody within a twenty yard radius of the boiler house before the air cleared and the stove returned to negative equity.

But that was not all. As I began to resemble some blacked up comedian about to imitate Al Jolsen singing 'Mammy', my comrades complained bitterly that the water for washing remained cold. It was a great relief when it was realised that my intelligent looks were not commensurate with my pyrogenic abilities and I was relieved of my command.

If the boiler house had its limitations, the toilets had a unique feature. The urinals had the usual fragrant aroma of such establishments, but the main problem of human wastage disposal, which had been at least partly solved by William Crapper's nineteenth century invention of the water closet, had an entirely different solution.

A large pipe, about two feet in diameter, ran along the back of the toilets. On the top of the pipe some six wide holes had been made, over which a wooden seat had been fitted. Between each sitting there was a small flimsy partition, but doors were conspicuous by their absence. Hence, men sat perched on the pipe in similar fashion to a group of crows taking their positions on telegraph wires. We may have been privates, but of privacy there was none.

The situation was, of course, fitting for lavatory-type humour and impromptu farting contests. However, every so often all talk would be brought to a halt by a sudden sluice of water, as all incumbents found themselves sitting a few inches above a minor tidal wave of faeces and miscellaneous items of jetsam. If anybody was in doubt as to where the associated draught had originated, he was acutely aware of where it was going.

In 1842, the British nation had been shaken by Edwin Chadwick's *Report on the Sanitary Conditions of the Labouring Population of Great Britain*. In the report, Chadwick had condemned the open sewers that were a common feature of town life throughout the country. If, one hundred years after his report, Chadwick's ghost had wandered around our camp, I am sure he would have turned his nose up at the Amersham arrangements.

Indeed, I have often mused on the body odours we must have emitted. None of us had any nightwear; we slept in the shirts and underpants that we had worn during the day. Such items were sent to the laundry but once a week. There were no sheets, and blankets were exchanged about every two months; nor were there pillows or pillowcases. Men would usually sleep with their heads rested on rolled-up denim overalls that they had worn all day. Showers or baths were usually on a weekly basis, although there were occasional opportunities for more frequent ablutions. As for socks, some pairs could stand upright by themselves and, had an NCO barked the right order, I am sure that they could have marched out of the hut by themselves.

The problems of body odours were exacerbated by the fact that two days of the week were 'doubling days'. On these occasions, all movements during parade hours had to be carried out at the double. As it was summer and the area of the camp was hilly, a reasonable amount of sweat would be exuded.

Dental inspections were rare and opportunities for late night cleaning of teeth were difficult or non-existent. Add all this up and it was remarkable that even our best friends did not tell us. Perhaps their own odours were worse, and one can only boggle at how men in action fared. How did the men fighting in thirty to forty degrees of frost in the various areas of conflict attend to their calls of nature? Reports are now to hand that men on the eastern front did not change their underwear for months, and were often crawling with lice, a little treat from which most British combatants were spared. In such theatres, no doubt the Amersham pipe would have been a model of hygiene.

Maps and Motorbikes

After the numerous questionnaires and interviews to which I had been subjected since enlistment, the powers-that-be suddenly realised that I was a reasonably experienced motorcyclist. So, after a brief test, I was designated the platoon's DR (dispatch rider), a post I was to occupy until I literally rode into the German's range of fire the following summer.

There were, of course, some marked differences between riding a motorcycle around the streets of London and my new duties. I had to learn the skills of cross-country riding: to negotiate steep descents and cater for thick mud. It was quite frightening to be astride a motorbike and have to rely on the gears of the machine – and one's nerve – to prevent a most rapid descent to the bottom of a hill vying for mountain status.

Although the winter weather in wartime London was grim, the Post Office deliveries that I had undertaken involved comparatively short journeys. But some army manoeuvres in which I was destined to become involved went on for weeks, and there was no cosy office to return to with the chances of warming up with a cup of hot tea.

DRs were subjected to the delights of map-reading and the mysteries of coordinates. With the ability to pinpoint one's position, how could one get lost? Only too easily. I do not know whether or not the wartime removal of road signs would have confused any invading army, but their absence certainly confused me.

There were numerous advantages in being a DR. One could often get away from the routine of camp life, and my appreciation of the Buckinghamshire countryside was enhanced by the running of messages to pleasant destinations. Spells of that great delight, guard duty, were reduced by the preferable duty DR responsibilities.

In August, I enjoyed my third leave, which was a very low-key affair. No friends were at home and nothing important seemed to be happening. There were rumours of Hitler's secret weapons, but we had heard all this before. What we did not know was that the RAF reconnaissance planes had obtained the first evidence of the V1 flying bomb that was to wreak havoc in London and southern England less than a year later.

As I walked back to the camp, from leave, I wondered what was going to happen next. For several weeks, nothing much did happen. Double summer time meant that it did not get dark until very late and the fine weather encouraged walking to the local cinema. I still remember a wonderful piece of Hollywood escapism called, *Hello 'Frisco, Hello*. The film featured Alice Faye, whose song, 'You'll Never Know Just How Much I Love You' hit the sentimental centre.

Often when in Amersham, I would visit the Sycamore Club. This was one of the many voluntary centres that had sprung up throughout the country to provide light refreshments to members of the forces at very low prices. All the helpers gave their services voluntarily and they were extremely friendly. No doubt some of the young lady helpers were happy to meet men folk, but there was a strong element of selflessness among the volunteers. Whether they received sufficient thanks for their efforts is questionable, but they certainly deserved the gratitude that was felt towards them.

Another form of escapism was to visit the local pub, The Magpies, was within a stone's throw of the camp and in a very pleasant rural setting. But, as funds were always low, visits were comparatively rare. The pub is still in its rural setting, but it now has an extension and a popular restaurant facility.

Although there was a two-mile walk to the station, which is right on the top of Amersham-on-the-Hill, going home on a Sunday was a popular pursuit. This gave rise to competition concerning who could swindle London Transport most effectively and make the return journey for the lowest price. Platform tickets and bookings to the next station down the line were common methods of duplicity, and back in barracks men would boast of how little they paid for their excursions. There was always some smart-arse who could undercut the others and give detailed accounts of his manoeuvres. Indeed, I awaited a claim that the transport company had paid a man to make the journey.

Much of this fiddling was only a farce, for the smart-arses were not so very clever. In reality, many ticket inspectors and bus conductors, especially the female 'clippies', had relatives in the forces, so they often turned a blind eye to the malpractices occurring, or only seemed to believe the unbelievable claims of where journeys were supposed to have started.

A more formidable obstacle to lightning visits home was the Military Police. But, as these upholders of military law tended to concentrate their activities at main line stations, the chances of being stopped on the London Underground were slender. I can remember being stopped only three times during my time in the army and these were when I was on official leave. Once in central London, when I was in civilian clothes, the detective who stopped me explained that he had done so because of my military bearing. As nothing could have been further from the truth, I realised that even policemen have their sense of humour.

It was at Amersham that I experienced my first taste of army justice, when I was placed on a charge for some minor misdemeanour. I forget the 'crime' that I had committed, but I shall never forget the pantomime that ensued. When one was charged, one was ordered 'cap off, quick march' and led into the company office under escort. Here one had to stand rigidly to attention before the company commander. The reason for the restriction on headwear, I understand, dated back to the time when soldiers wore heavy dress helmets and convicted men, possibly sentenced to some hundred lashes, were reputed to have thrown their helmets at the officer. By 1943, corporal punishment had long been abolished and it was mainly mental punishment that prevailed, so hurling a forage cap in retaliation for the awarded sentence was scarcely an effective countermeasure. But if the punishments had changed, the ritual of arraignment seems to have prevailed. In 1943, no criminal facing charges of mass murder would have encountered similar intimidating indictment proceedings.

When the accused had been lined up before the officer, the NCO making the charge would take one pace forward, banging his boots on the floor as he did so. He would then salute and shout out some hackneyed spiel such as, 'Sir, at 0800 hours I observed the accused doing so and so, I ordered him to stop and he said rhubarb, rhubarb, rhubarb…So I placed him under open arrest, SIR!' Then more saluting and banging of feet.

At the conclusion of this pantomime, the accused would then be invited to have his say before the matter was settled. The accused could, of course, have been highly confused by the rigmarole and, if he were inarticulate, would have had great difficulty in arguing his case. Nobody, unless one opted for a court martial, had the right to appoint another person to speak for him. But some of the lads who were familiar with the arraign-ment procedures did not need anybody to speak for them. Indeed, some of the explanations for the defence would have left Portia looking like a junior partner to the late Horace Rumpole. The officer presiding, if he had any sense of justice, had to decide between the improbable and impossible as weird and wonderful excuses were spluttered forth.

One man explained that his late return to camp was due to the fact that, as he was about to commence his return journey, his father came back into the family home drunk and started to strike his mother. How could any true Englishman leave his battered mum to fend for herself? Unfortunately for the accused, he told his story a little too convincingly, for the officer wanted to inform the police of this violent character. It required a great deal of backtracking to convince the captain that the accused father's action was a one-off affair and highly unlikely to recur. Later, the accused informed me that his father was only a moderate drinker and was never known to be violent to anybody, let alone his wife.

As for my charge, I was lucky. Undoubtedly my experience of arguing on political matters helped me a lot, and I was let off with a reprimand.

Of course, one could rail at the army's system of justice, but all criticisms fade into insignificance if comparisons are made with events in Europe, where summary executions made sentences of being confined to barracks seem very small beer.

Italy Falls, but Not Far Enough!

On an evening trip to Amersham in early September, the news broke that Mussolini had been overthrown and that the new Italian government had asked for an armistice. Naturally, spirits rose as we envisaged the Allies gaining easy access to Germany via the back door. Alas, the German army moved with considerable speed; Mussolini was daringly rescued from his captors and the fighting settled down to a slow and bloody slog up the boot of Italy. How many lives were then lost because of the rivalry between British and American army commanders is incalculable.

It was obvious that, in our neck of the War, changes were bound to occur. In mid-September, our colonel told the battalion that we were to become part of the 15th Scottish Division and that the major general in command would be appearing next week to welcome us. This, of course, involved the complementary piece of bull in the form of a rehearsal for the general's inspection. Included in the rehearsal was the order to 'off caps and three cheers for the general'. Naturally, with nobody there to cheer, the response was minimal. The colonel was furious. 'Great God,' he exploded, 'I could shout louder than that myself!' So for the next ten minutes we had to practice cheering a non-existent general.

Of great interest to us was the news that we would shortly be moving to the Leeds area of Yorkshire and that, within a short time of our arrival, we would be going out on the moors for three weeks' manoeuvres. Preparations for the move were to begin immediately.

And so, on 30 September – I remember the date because it was my mother's birthday and I had forgotten to send her a card – we moved out from Amersham. As a DR, it was my lot to help shepherd the convoy of vehicles and perform point duties where necessary. Being a DR in such circumstances had distinct advantages, for whereas most of the troops were confined to their trucks, DRs could easily stop at roadside cafés and partake of refreshment.

We left at the crack of dawn and, late that afternoon, arrived in the town of Otley, which is about ten miles from Leeds. This brought General Rommel and me a little closer together.

Otley: Gateway to the Moors and Misery

As I tottered from my motorbike on arrival in the town, my immediate impression of Otley was that this was where they must have made the film *Love on the Dole*; a film based upon Walter Greenwood's novel of life in an industrial town during the depression of the 1930s. The weather was dull and grey and so were the buildings. The town was small, with a population of about ten thousand. It had a cinema, a large number of pubs, and a YMCA, but very little else.

Just outside of town were Farley Barracks, which were used to accommodate the Scots battalions of the division, but support units such as ours were quartered in odd spots in the town centre. Most of my company was billeted on the top floor of a huge furniture depository, which we immediately christened the 'ballroom'. The story circulated that the top floor had been condemned for the storage of furniture, but was deemed good enough for troops. How true this was is uncertain, but the army's love of bull, with its insistence that all beds should be lined up and clothing hung in strict order, was ruined when it rained – as it frequently did. Then, hasty rearrangements had to be made to stop the cascades from the leaking roof ruining equipment.

The top floor of the ballroom had two sections and was home to about forty men. Access was via a single doorway with an adjoining rickety wooden staircase on the outside of the building and a stone staircase on the inside which, during night-time, was completely black. At the bottom of these staircases were the mod cons, which comprised about a dozen washbasins, complete with running cold water, and about the same number of toilets. A common expression for men anxious to urinate was that they were 'breaking their neck for a piss'. This description of their plight often nearly came true, as manoeuvres at night on a windswept exterior staircase, or a spine-breaking tumble on the stone interior steps, were distinct possibilities. Bearing in mind the need to maintain blackout restrictions, lighting everywhere was at a minimum. I shudder to think what would have happened had there been a fire and a mad dash for the single doorway had ensued.

To the north of Otley is the Chevin, a hill vying for mountain status, which was to send its abundant rain water cascading down to flood the entrance to our billets. This proved another blow to the life of bull, for how could one look smart when puddle-jumping from one dry patch of land to another?

As the Yorkshire winter strengthened, the question of heating became more important. There were a couple of pot-bellied stoves in the billet, but we had no allocation of fuel. Hence we had to 'win' our supplies of combustible material, which put anything that would burn in great danger.

My acquaintance with northern England before my Otley days had been very limited; now I was to receive a number of surprises. Apart from the expected Yorkshire accent, there were the different expressions. Being 'fair-starved' meant one was cold, and those pleased with life were 'laughing clog hats'. Many things and people were 'champion'. Although Yorkshire people had a reputation of being over-careful with their money, the inhabitants of Otley were very kind to us servicemen and generous in many ways.

Workers going to the factories still wore clogs, which in the early morning sounded like an army on the march. In the pubs, the dartboards had no treble ring, nor outer bull's-eye. But the beer was good – really good – and in marked contrast to the wartime brews of southern England.

So on our first night in Otley, a Saturday, many of the lads went to one of the many pubs and imbibed the limited quantity of beer that army pay allowed. After only two pints of Tetley's or John Smith's Magnet Ales, whose strength was in marked contrast to the customary weak southern brews, an unexpected degree of leglessness was experienced. To say that we stumbled back to our billets was an inadequate description of the scene. Of course, we had our member of the awkward squad with us; namely, one Henry Cossins, who took a stumble too far and landed face down in the stream just outside our billet. But help was at hand and Henry was manhandled up the stairs, where he was dumped unceremoniously on his bed and a blanket thrown over him. Next morning Henry's immediate neighbours were startled to hear him cry, 'I'm blind, I've gone blind!'

At this stage of the War, there was a shortage of alcoholic drinks in many parts of the country. Servicemen and others in lonely spots were liable to experience severe restrictions of supplies, with the result that some desperate addicts would resort to drinking weird brews – especially wood-alcohol. The results were sometimes devastating, including madness and blindness. Thus, our dear Henry, having perhaps only the vaguest idea of what he had imbibed the night before, leapt to the conclusion that he had drunk himself into the realm of permanent darkness.

The response to Henry's *cri-de-coeur* was touching. His nearby neighbours could see that, owing to his aquatic antics of the previous evening, a thin film of mud from the stream was covering the lens of his glasses. A barrage of verbal abuse met Henry's cry for help, among which the advice to 'wipe the shit off your specs, you stupid bastard' proved to be one of the kindest offerings.

It was on a Monday Morning

By the Monday we had fully explored the town's meagre amenities and begun to appreciate the importance of the YMCA, which offered refreshments and a place to sit in reasonable comfort. But we were not in Otley to drink tea and, without too much enthusiasm, training was resumed.

There was no suitable parade ground in Otley and, as we were a mechanised unit, it was natural that much of our time should be taken up with the maintenance of our vehicles: lightly-armoured twin-tracked Bren Gun carriers, fifteen cwt trucks, jeeps, and motorcycles. A feature of the water-cooled engines in most of these vehicles was that, because antifreeze fluid was not available, in wintertime all such vehicles had to be drained at the end of the day and refilled with water before they could be used again. Hence, if a large number of vehicles were to move off at the same time, as at the beginning of a scheme, considerable delays were involved before a start could be made.

70

Otley boasted a famous rugby club, and in 1943 its car park was used to harbour our vehicles, whilst the changing facilities became the guardroom. At the time, the premises were alive with mice and off duty sentries were lulled to sleep by a cacophony of squeaking. Each evening a particular worker wending his way home would present the sentry on the gate with a packet of fish and chips. This kindness was most appreciated, and we wondered if the same menu was the nightly supper of the donor.

The character of guard duty was made more interesting by a tragedy. A young member of the company called Wilks was an obvious misfit. His very appearance and lack of understanding of whether it was two o'clock or Thursday left him open to much verbal bullying. He should never have been in the army.

One night, when on guard duty, Wilks could take it no more. So he went round to the back of the guard room, put the barrel of his rifle in his mouth and pulled the trigger. The ever-watchful guard slept on, blissfully unaware of the noise of the shot until it was Wilk's turn to go on stag (watch) again.

Apart from the tragedy to the Wilk's family, there was another unfortunate occurrence. By mistake, the next-of-kin of a man called Willes received a telegram: 'We regret to inform you that your son has committed suicide'. Poor Mrs Willes, the next of kin, nearly had a heart attack.

If men of the company had been asked whether or not they believed in ghosts, most would have replied in the negative, including myself. But, in the small hours of the morning, in the darkness of the car park when there were all kinds of drippings, and flappings from the vehicles, I must confess that my Marxist materialist beliefs were often tested. On one occasion I felt the hairs on the back of my neck rise when a stray cat suddenly leapt down from one of the trucks. Confidence was not increased when men going on guard were warned, 'Beware, Wilks walks tonight!'

What about the War?

As we cavorted about in Otley, most of us knew that there could be no Second Front in 1943, but that it was almost certain that it would be attempted the following year. On the eastern front, the Germans were retreating. Smolensk, capital of the Ukraine, had been liberated at the end of September and the Allies were advancing, albeit slowly and under great difficulties, in Italy. Although we did not know it at the time, British Intelligence was carefully monitoring German steps to build launching sites for the V1 and V2 rockets, which were to plague Britain the following year. The situation in the Far East was encouraging as Japan was forced more and more on to the defensive.

Obviously many of these facts were unknown to us, and most of us did not even know where Smolensk was. None could foresee what a bitter storm of retribution was building against the German population, as Soviet forces maintained their offensive. After their victory at Kursk, the Red Army began to advance towards the Polish border, and shortly afterwards upon Germany itself. I think it fair to say that we were more concerned with the mundane matter of keeping warm.

One matter was not mundane, for it was another minor tragedy. The ballroom was situated about 200 yards from the cookhouse and on the main road to Leeds. Each morning, we would line up and march along the road to where breakfast awaited us. But, as British summertime was maintained throughout the year and doubled at the height of summer, it did not get light until quite late in the morning. Hence, the march to breakfast was held in the dark.

One terrible morning, with the blackout playing havoc with road lighting, a bus on its way to Leeds ploughed into the back of the column. The warning lamp that should have been carried was simply not there, and in the poor light the bus driver was unaware of what lay before him.

It was a terrible situation: one man was killed and several injured, which in the circumstances was a fairly light toll. Sometime in the mid-1950s, a similar accident occurred in Chatham when a bus ploughed into a group of marching army cadets. This case hit the headlines, but our tragedy passed largely unnoticed. Following our accident, we were allowed to make our individual way to the canteen.

The weather was proving poor and we were hardly bursting with enthusiasm as we prepared for the three weeks scheme about which we had been warned before we left Amersham. But then I was smitten by a complaint that made me look like a fugitive from a leper colony: impetigo. Sleeping with dirty denim overalls for a pillow was exacting its price.

Impetigo is a condition involving a nasty series of sores that are highly contagious, so at the time when the battalion was ordered out on to the moors, I was ordered into a cottage hospital in the famous town of song, Ilkley. Together with several other sufferers, we were kept in quarantine and our faces painted with a purple dye that made us look like candidates for a grand Halloween party. But at least we enjoyed clean sheets and warm accommodation until our appearances returned to something like normal.

When I returned to Otley, most of the company were still on the moors, and I was given a suspiciously friendly welcome from the sergeant in charge of the rear party. 'Richards,' he only half shouted at me, 'I've got a special job for you.' My heart sank, surely I was not going to be nominated boiler man again as I had been so disastrously at Amersham. 'You are to be the Duty DR for the next five days.'

This meant that I was to remain near the company office all day, sleep in the guardroom, and be ready to run any necessary messages. In addition, the DR was roused about 5 a.m. in order to make the early morning calls to personnel, such as the cooks, who were billeted around the town.

Once again I was reminded of *Love on the Dole*, which contained scenes of people known as 'knockers-up' who walked or cycled around their patch, waking workers for their day in the mill or factory by tapping on their windows. Why such workers had not invested in alarm clocks has puzzled me ever since. I could understand army cooks not having alarm clocks, but not industrial workers whose wages may have been poor, but would surely stretch to such an investment.

Shortly after all the company had returned from the moors, we were ordered to attend for dental inspections. There were no cosmetic considerations to army dentistry. If you had sufficient molars to be able to eat, dentures were denied no matter how you looked with front teeth missing. No anaesthetics were used for fillings and extractions were carried out on a conveyor belt system. Luckily I had to lose only one tooth. A clumsily inserted needle was pushed into my gums, then I was ordered from the chair until several other sufferers were dealt with in similar fashion. Then back to the chair for some brutal yanking that left me feeling like I had been given a good hiding. Fortunately this was my last encounter with such masters of dental care.

A Foggy Leave in London Town

In early November, almost a year to the day I had joined the army, I emerged from a very sooty King's Cross station in London to enjoy ten whole days of freedom.

I had two aims in mind: one, to have some good nights with two of my drinking partners, the other, to try to woo a certain young lady. I succeeded only too well in the first objective, but failed only too badly in the second. The lady in question just would not woo – at least not with me.

Luck was with me, for my old friend Roly was home on leave and my cousin Nobby was in a reserved occupation and always happy to drink with friends of yesteryear. So we quickly adjourned to a pub and, as the drinks flowed, we could see ever more clearly how the War could be won and what idiots the generals were. Naturally we had no idea of the Enigma machine and the work of some of the best brains in the country at Bletchley Park.

In our kangaroo court, we had condemned in their absence most of our war leaders, when a young man from the family group sitting at the next table approached us. He gestured towards his mother, who smiled at us, before explaining that my friend Roly, who was in naval uniform, reminded his mum of his elder brother George, who was also in the navy and whose birthday it was that day. George was serving somewhere at sea, so he wondered if Roly would kindly deputise for him and would we all have a drink in George's honour?

How could we refuse such a heart-rending request? One toast to George quickly led to another, but, as closing time was called, I remember having a distinct worry: I had been drinking for some hours, but still felt strangely sober. The moment we walked into the cold night air, the results were disastrous.

Just outside of our drinking hole was another drinking hole; a horse trough. These troughs were still fairly common in London as there was still a limited amount of horse drawn traffic about. As our legs suddenly developed minds of their own, circumnavigating a way around the trough in question necessitated very careful planning.

Slowly we lurched our way to Nobby's house which luckily was nearby. We tottered inside where Nobby's mother, my aunt, did her best to guide us to the bathroom and then allowed us to collapse on sofas and armchairs. As I lay wondering if death would not be a preferable option, my aunt would insist on asking us if we would like a cup of cocoa. Fond as I was of the good lady, for I had known her all my life, I wished that she had had suggested cyanide instead.

The next day I was not my brightest, nor best, and for the first time in years glasses of water became strangely attractive.

Then the days began to speed up considerably and I became lost in a whirl of political meetings, and trips to the cinema. But before my return I decided to visit my first place of work and talk to the man who had been in charge of us lads in the dim distant time when I was only 14 years of age.

Mr Thwaites was still at his desk and he welcomed me most warmly. Ted, as he was secretly referred to by us lads, had lost his left arm in the First World War, he was a disciplinarian, and a Tory to boot. Why on earth should I want to go and see him?

The main reason was that he was very fair in any of the penalties he administered, he could appreciate different points of view, and he was the sort of person that one could turn to for advice. He had a kind of wisdom that was derived not only from books. Some sixty years later I can still remember our discussion, his views on how the War could be won, and his searching questions to me as to my future career. Ted certainly gave me much to think about. But then I had to think about saying farewell to friends and parents and wending my way, like the reluctant schoolboy on his way to school, back up north.

Now is the Winter of our Discontent

And so, in the middle of November, I caught an early afternoon train to Leeds and then on to my favourite Yorkshire town. On the way up I shared a compartment with a civilian who turned out to be a local secretary of his branch of the Workers Education Association and we discussed the rapidly changing international situation.

His comments made me aware of gaps in my grasp of affairs and I resolved to make more effort with the basic general education correspondence course I had been following, courtesy of an arrangement between my civilian life trade union and Ruskin College at Oxford.

When one returned from leave there was always the delight of a spell of guard duty and other onerous tasks which made life so very jolly. One evening with such pleasant prospects before me, I decided to take a stroll. It was already dark when suddenly in one of the back streets of the town I burst into tears. For several minutes I just sobbed.

Although I can be emotionally moved by the plight of other people, especially children, I rarely shed tears on my own behalf; big boys simply do not cry. With a feeling of shame, I began to remonstrate with myself. What the hell was I doing crying like a baby? I was not hungry, cold, nor wet; I was not facing death every night as were our bomber crews, nor was I in danger of the perils of the sea. Why, then, was I proving such a wimp?

Naturally, I could not begin to rationalise immediately, but as I walked on and gradually made my way to a cup of tea in a quiet corner in the YMCA I began to formulate some answers. The hard fact was that I, like so many other people, was war weary. The prevailing conflict had been raging for just over four years, as long as the First World War, and although it was fairly certain that the Axis powers could not win, the end of hostilities seemed a long way away. The Second Front had yet to be opened, and afterwards there was the murderous prospect of island-hopping towards the mainland of Japan. I was nineteen years old at the time of my tearful interlude. How old would I be, assuming I was fortunate enough to survive, before the War ended? And if I did survive would I be in one piece?

But another conflict was closer to hand; namely, the company's boxing competition. It was a form of escapism that induced me to put my name down, for entrants were excused a number of parades and duties and were able to concentrate on matters other than army bullshit. Also, I welcomed the opportunity to sweat the beer out of my system. Running up the Chevin was a good way of getting fit.

There was, of course, the excitement and the fear of climbing into the ring and meeting opponents who always looked much bigger and tougher than oneself. Despite my earlier bout of the blues, I was able to reach the final of my weight before a very tough fight witnessed my defeat. I left the ring with a badly swollen lip.

Clacton Capers

It was now getting close to Christmas, and the army decided that it would give us a pre-festive present. We were to go to Clacton-on-Sea, not to make sandcastles, but to practise firing our Polsten guns at a moving target. An ancient plane designed by the Wright brothers was to pull a windsock behind it and fly about a quarter of a mile out to sea, parallel to the coast. We would be on the beach firing at the sock, which promised to be even more entertaining than building sandcastles.

My services as a DR were not required on the journey and I travelled to Clacton in the back of a fifteen cwt truck. The vehicle had no heating, although the driver and his front seat passenger derived some warmth from the engine. We in the back had only our greatcoats, which left us very cold indeed. After the War, I learned of the manner in which various groups of people were forced into unheated railway cattle compartments, with little food and no hygiene facilities, and driven for days without any organised breaks – usually to their deaths. Accounts of such episodes make my Clacton trip seem like a luxury excursion.

Clacton was in what was known as a 'defence area'. Most civilians had been evacuated and we were accommodated in empty houses whose owners had gone to safer regions. The beach had been mined in most places and guns bristled everywhere. When night fell, the place was like a ghost town of Wild West fame. Many shops were boarded up and those that were open did very little business. But our business was to shoot down, or at least ladder, the elusive windsocks.

However, before we were permitted to fire, we were given various instructions. We were told to aim several yards in front of the sock so that both shell and sock should meet. Any man who fired too far in front of the sock and shot the plane down would be on an immediate charge. All hell broke loose when the plane made its first run and some six or seven guns opened up as the plane slowly chugged its way against the prevailing wind. But the sock seemed to be in its virgin condition and entirely free from violation.

Then came the turn of 'Snowball' Barker (so-called because of his exceedingly fair hair). Barker was a bit of a wideboy and had an answer for most people in authority. He threw theory to the wind and aimed his gun directly at the target with the result that the tracer shells indicated a number of hits. When the officer in charge went over to congratulate Barker on his fine shooting, the look on Snowball's face made it clear that he was expecting a bollocking for disobeying instructions and not firing in the prescribed fashion.

Each morning we trooped down to the beach and each morning the sock survived; only the nerves of the pilot concerned were in tatters. In the afternoons we were given lectures on the mechanism of the gun and general information on aircraft tactics. But the army being the army had to throw in bouts of drill, so what few civilians remained in the area were startled to hear boots marching up and down and incomprehensible orders being shouted by leather-lunged NCOs.

On Sunday there had to be a church parade, so we all filed into the local place of worship. In the congregation were a number of civilians, one of whom objected to our presence. At intervals he would interject with religious slogans such as 'Blessed are the peacemakers' and 'Thou shall not kill'. He protested when he was asked to leave. 'Very well,' he cried, 'I shall quit the house of the Lord.'

I felt like giving him a clap as he departed. What struck me as an atheist was the humbug of God being on our side and, according to the German chaplains, their side as well. I believed that the War against Nazi Germany had to be won, but the idea that the killing involved should receive some holy blessing was one that I could not accept.

As the firing practice course was coming to an end, the news broke that Sir Oswald Mosley, leader of the British Union of Fascists and would-be Führer of Britain, had been released from jail, where he had been held since 1940 under Section 18b of the Defence Regulations. The reasons given were that he was a sick man and that prison was causing his health to deteriorate. Under the conditions of his release, it was argued, he would not be able to do anything to hinder the war effort.

This action, by the then Home Secretary, Herbert Morrison, caused a storm of political protest. One could not do much in Clacton-on-Sea, but I was able to organise a successful petition and collection, which was sent to the *Daily Worker*, the Communist Party's newspaper.

Little did I know, when I was collecting signatures and cash, that some four years later I would be one of a team of speakers in Ridley Road protesting at the 'desperately ill' Mosley seeking to bring his racially motivated Union Movement into the East End of London. Some thirteen years after this, 1959, Mosley was fit enough to stand as a Parliamentary candidate in the General Election, although this time his racial target was Black people instead of Jews.

It was Christmas Eve in the Millpond

Three days before Christmas, our company commander told us that we would be leaving Clacton at noon the following day, provided all the necessary cleaning had been done to our billets. This was good news, for the idea of spending the holiday in the gloom of a ghost town was hardly an attractive proposition. Also, many of the lads had their Otley girlfriends, or had 'their feet under the table' somewhere in the town. And so began the return journey; the only trouble was that it had got much colder and I was not sorry that I was not on my motorbike.

When we had travelled about a third of the way back to Otley, we stopped for the night at the same disused mill at which we had stopped on the way down. Early in the morning, we were awakened from our lumpy floorboard repose to face another refrigerated journey, but of course we had first to attend to our ablutions. Down to the adjacent pond we trooped, where we scooped up handfuls of ice-cold brackish water, which we splashed rather sparingly on our faces. On our arrival back in Otley, our brown-stained countenances suggested that we had returned from the Middle East rather than Essex. Every Christmas Eve since that year, I have remembered the joys of paddling in the millpond.

The rest of our journey back was brightened up by workers, who had finished early, giving us a warm cheer as they gathered at pub doorways. Back we came to a town bathed in mid-winter darkness, but with an abundance of pubs. At least we were not being shot at and we were able to wash and shave in clean cold running water.

Christmas Day that year was on a Saturday and so there was an extended weekend holiday. Of course, on Christmas Day itself there was the ritual of a church parade, when a host of hung-over men trooped in to go through the business of worship. It was more a case of silent curses than 'Silent Night'. However, our flagging spirits were revived when we 'marched' off in a most unmilitary manner to a splendid dinner.

Army food had a reputation for being unpalatable, but we were lucky in having a corporal cook who was most conscientious, and we had a very good meal indeed. During the repast, our colonel came round to wish us a Merry Christmas. He hoped that by next year we would be home with our families, and for once we all agreed with him. Unfortunately, his predictions were to prove markedly optimistic.

As several days of comparative idleness passed by, more time was spent in bed or helping with a party organised for the local children. Naturally, the more pleasant jobs, such as being Father Christmas, went to the officers; for one horrible moment I thought that the poor kids would have to salute before they received their gifts.

Just before the holiday ended, our captain wandered into the billet to tell us that Germany's one remaining battlecruiser, the *Scharnhorst*, had been sunk. This victory was seen as a most acceptable Christmas present. The complete elimination of the German surface fleet had occurred when Allied shipping losses from enemy submarines were declining dramatically and gave great hope for the Battle of the Atlantic.

By the Friday of the holiday week we were all desperately short of cash, and pay parade could not have come a moment too soon. Unfortunately, in the excitement of the occasion I left my rifle in the outer section of the company office. The sergeant major was not at all pleased and, in army parlance, did his nut. 'Richards,' he stormed, 'you can thank your ancestors that it's New Year's Eve, otherwise you'd have been on a real right fizzer.' I mumbled various words of apologies and thanks and slunk away to lick my wounds from his verbal onslaught. Had he put me on a charge, the new year would have started on a very grim note.

It was remarkable how quickly one's assessment of the War's progress changed. In my blue mood of November, I was distressed at the prospect of still wearing khaki for many years to come. But naturally the end of the year was a time to reflect on the progress made in the previous twelve months. On every front the Axis powers had been retreating and there seemed little chance of this process being reversed. The big question for us lads was when we would begin the retreat from Otley and start to advance, hopefully, into Europe. 1944 was to provide the answer.

1944: Let's Get On with It!

A few days into the new year and a minor bombshell hit us. We were told that General Montgomery, as he then was, had decided that he would have too much light anti-aircraft cover for the oncoming invasion and, as a result, my section would have to switch from Polsten guns to the Vickers machine-gun. Obviously our many hours of aircraft recognition and our mid-winter trip to Clacton were surplus to requirements. Some transfer of men to the Scots Regiments, the Gordon Highlanders, the Seaforth Highlanders and other units would be necessary.

The issue of transfers caused considerable debate, for the Scots battalions were infantry, whereas the Middlesex Regiment, albeit officially infantry, was mechanised and intended to give machine gun and mortar support to those who were to do the attacking. However, as no orders for movement were immediately forth-coming, the debate temporarily subsided into the background; we were back to the delights of life in the ballroom.

In later years, I learned of the meticulous planning that had gone into the invasion of Normandy, but obviously this was not known at this stage. As a result, most of us cursed at the boring routine and wished that the brass hats would make up their bloody minds.

As Christmas faded into the mists of memory and routine resumed, there was a marked lack of enthusiasm during parade hours. In the biting cold weather that came down from the hills, routine maintenance and the cleaning of vehicles was distinctly unpleasant. But to slope off to a local cafe was dangerous, lest some prowling NCO should wander in on the bun fight. I then had a seemingly brilliant idea. At the top of the Chevin, lost in the mists and snow and looking like a scene from *Wuthering Heights*, was a café; surely nobody would look for us there! I put this master escape plan to my friend Rufus, whose crime sheets were reaching voluminous proportions, and he jumped at the sugges-tion. And so we trudged to the top of this near mountain – which must be a close cousin of Everest – for a well-earned cup of char.

Unfortunately we had a provost sergeant, who on occasions had been seen weeping into his beer as he bemoaned the fact that flogging in the army had been abandoned during the nineteenth century. Whether or not he had followed us to the summit I shall never know, but he seemed very pleased to see us – a feeling not reciprocated. He ordered us down to town, our tea unfinished, with a satisfied smirk that indicated he had found two candidates for the chain gang. Naturally, we were both on a charge.

How was I to get out of this one? When all the banging and shouting that is part of the process of a charge had finished, I was asked if I had anything to say in mitigation. Obviously I could not deny the facts and so I pleaded that I was just recovering from a severe cold; a brisk walk to the top of the Chevin and a cup of hot tea afterwards would prevent a relapse and the need for me to report sick the following day. I realised that I had committed an offence, but I thought that I had done my best both for the company and myself. The officer trying the case pondered and for one awful moment I wondered if I were to face an additional charge of taking the piss. But, much to my relief, he accepted my account and with a few words of warning he dismissed the case.

But what about my friend Rufus? Unfortunately, Rufus had two things going against him. First, the story which he had concocted was not very convincing, secondly the length of his crime sheet was fatal. He was given seven days' 'jankers'. Rufus bore me no resentment, but the provost sergeant was furious; I was careful to steer well clear of him as long as I could.

This was not too difficult as we were destined to start a four week scheme and our unit would be scattered to the three Ridings of Yorkshire.

Out in the Cold, Cold Snow

As the winter days lengthened and the cold strengthened, the scheme began. On very icy roads my unit set off from Otley going to no-one knew where. Snow lay on the moor and every pool of water was frozen solid. And there was I, perched on my motorbike, feeling very isolated and anxious not to swerve lest the bike go one way and me another.

We went through some remote villages with peculiar names; 'Blubber-Houses' comes readily to mind. But came the hour when blundering about around Blubber Houses was becoming increasingly dangerous and into a snow-covered field we camped down for the night. When the several coatings of snow had been removed from the surface we discovered ground as hard as granite. But with dextrous use of ground sheets, tarpaulins, and vehicles we sought to make some sort of home. Mod cons were sadly lacking.

On the first night we had no problems regarding being near to the food truck, but as the scheme progressed our paths tended to go in different directions. Indeed, while the brass hats were learning important lessons in logistics, we lesser mortals were learning how to manoeuvre ourselves as near as possible to comfortable positions and, of course, the food truck. I sometimes had brief feelings of guilt; were these desires to be near to bodily comforts in the best spirit of winning the War? Were we more interested in drinking tea than killing Germans?

Perhaps there are no conclusive answers to these questions. Certainly we wanted to win the War, but accounts of battles and works of fiction based on fact point to the abilities of front line men to look after themselves in the most trying of circumstances. Artefacts dug up from the battle fields of the First World War indicate widespread attempts to make life as comfortable as possible in all the filth and dangers of the trenches. The Desert Rats of the Second World War were renowned for 'brewing up' for tea as well as winning the all-important Battle of El Alamein.

It would seem it was in the best traditions of warfare that a group of my comrades hit upon a brilliant idea to obtain some comforts, and this time there was no provost sergeant hovering in the background who had to be side-stepped. One evening when we were stuck in a cold, snow-covered field we were aware that there was a RAF airfield nearby. We knew that there would be a NAAFI on the site. So individually we made our way to the edge of our field, then walked in single file, patrol fashion, to the guarded gate of the airfield complex.

Our self-appointed 'patrol leader' then requested permission from the sentry for us to enter and use the NAAFI. Naturally the duty officer had to be consulted and he, bless him, agreed to our request. Luckily for him we were not a Nazi version of the *Dirty Dozen*. No doubt our pure London cockney accents and expressions were better proof of our origins than any supporting papers.

The powdered egg on toast, a favourite item of wartime cuisine, tasted delicious, and the decor and warmth of the building were in marked contrast to the frozen fields outside. But we dared not press our luck too far and with thanks to all concerned our 'patrol' returned in the same way as it came.

Could we use the same tactics the next night? I was given no such chance for I was ordered to maintain contact with an officer of one of the Scots battalions who, in the middle of the night, was being driven around the moors to liaise with other units. So for some three hours I slipped and slid around the pitch black moors wearing so many clothes that, when I dismounted from my bike, I could hardly move.

An advantage of being a DR on schemes was that it was very difficult for any umpire to detect which side I was on. All DRs had to wear the standard crash helmet, and the divisional signs that all vehicles displayed were almost impossible to paint on motorbikes. Hence, I had a fair degree of freedom to roam the moors without too much fear of being taken 'prisoner'.

Again, in the spirit of looking after home comforts, I was prevailed upon by my colleagues to visit local villages, when and where they existed, to try to buy cigarettes for them. Cigarettes were not rationed, but they were in short supply, so I was able to purchase only limited amounts. The retail price of a packet of twenty cigarettes was 1s. 6d. in old money, or 7.5p in today's currency. I am sure that if I had asked for 10s. (50p) a packet, a large sum in those days, I could have made a profit of nearly a quarter of my weekly pay. But, as I had been pointing out the evils of the capitalist world and the misery it was causing, I could not sell my principles so cheaply.

As the cold intensified and the snow deepened, it was hoped that the scheme would be called off. No such luck! The divisional commander decided that, in respect for the men fighting in Italy, the scheme would continue. Much as I wanted to return to the delights of Otley, I realised that the General was right. Although life on the moors was unpleasant, nobody was shooting at us and nobody was falling wounded only to freeze in sub-Arctic temperatures, as they were doing at Anzio and Cassino. And so the scheme dragged on and on and on.

But all bad things must come to an end and, at last, the news came through that the scheme would begin to wind down. At the end of February, the conquering heroes returned to the ballroom, happy to be out of the cold, but sober in the realisation that the real thing could not be far away.

Spring is Here Again

We may have been out of the cold, but the problem of the lack of toilet facilities – like the problem of the deserving poor – was still with us. Unfortunately, the timing of the demands of my friend Ken's bladder coincided exactly with the arrival of the orderly sergeant, who started to mount the exterior staircase below just as the cascade began. The sergeant was not amused, and neither was Ken when he was given seven days jankers.

Another urinary episode followed when the owner of the depository complained that the fire buckets that were overflowing by night were having a detrimental effect on the polish on the furniture stored below. In answer to this complaint, the company commander imposed a punishment guard upon the buckets in question.

I was, of course, one of the lucky few designated for the task. In regulation dress, tin hat, small pack and rifle, I stood for much of the night ready to open fire on any man with a message of desperation writ large on his face. Fortunately no massacre was necessary, for when the bleary-eyed, would-be miscreants were able to focus on my John Bull stance, they turned and blundered towards the door, their shirttails flapping in abject surrender. 'So what did you do in the Great War, Daddy?' 'I helped to save the fire buckets of Otley from serious misuse.'

The very next day after this fiasco, we were marched out to a nearby recreation ground to hear General Montgomery, who was making one of his famous tours of the troops. He told us what a fine body of men we were and how, with our latest weapons, we would have a great time on the mainland of Europe. If questions had been allowed, I would have agreed that our weapons were fine, but asked if perhaps we could now have somewhere to pee.

The Last Leave

It was time for another leave, and once again I inhaled the bracing air of King's Cross station. The leave proved to be enjoyable, but not very exciting. My cousin Nobby had at last been called up for the army, and my friend Roly was busy sinking Japanese ships in Far Eastern waters. Even the girl I had previously tried to woo had joined the Land Army and was busy growing potatoes in some distant field. So I had some time to visit the parents of friends of mine. They were always pleased to see me and it was a pleasure to exchange news.

I was unaware that this was to be my last full leave, for events behind the scenes were moving fast and some effects were soon to surface. The various commanders of the invading force were being appointed and letters home were now being censored. Many of the married men and those who were having passionate affairs went to great lengths to avoid their messages of love, lies, and desperation being read by the officers. Quite a lot of pub talk now concentrated upon Hitler's secret weapons. But nobody knew of the growing evidence about the V1s and V2s, which were the rockets that were to rain on Britain later in the year. Most people felt that they had enough on their hands with known wartime menaces, without speculating upon future horrors. It was just as well that ignorance was bliss.

What political meetings I was able to attend were reasonably free from heated controversy, for the main aim of all parties was to win the War. London was experiencing some air raids about this time, but none occurred while I was at home. In one such raid, a former workmate of mine, who had helped to organise my farewell party before I enlisted, was killed when a bomb hit his favourite dance hall. He was pulled from the rubble with the girl with whom he was dancing clasped in his arms.

So, in mid-March, and with the feeling that something spec-tacular was about to happen, I returned from leave to Otley.

Meanwhile, in the Far East, the Americans began to intensify their island-hopping towards Japan, but at a heavy cost in lives;

the scale of the American efforts and the importance of the aircraft carrier as a naval weapon only became clear after the War. In eastern Europe, the advance of the Red Army had been slowed while the Germans seemed more intent on killing Jews in the most horrendous fashion than on killing Russians.

Take your Partners for the Last Waltz

Then something did happen to my unit, though hardly of war-shaking proportions. We moved from the furniture depository we had long called the ballroom to a purpose-built military camp at Poole, situated about a quarter of a mile from Otley itself. We were then informed that our unit would not be in the first wave of the pending invasion and our task would be to consolidate the territory gained, following up accordingly. This news was welcomed, but we had no idea how bloody the following-up process was to prove.

Life in Poole was much more civilised than in the ballroom. Indeed, as the weather improved, the days became enjoyable. Concentration now centred upon weapon handling and battle tactics. But these matters were interrupted when we were told to prepare for a royal visit. King George VI and Queen Elizabeth would be passing nearby the following week and we were to be given the honour of marching some three miles before lining the road to cheer their majesties as they whisked by. I could hardly wait.

The great day came and off we marched to wait, and wait, and wait for the cavalcade, which eventually came thundering across the moorlands. A number of armoured cars, equipped with light anti-aircraft guns, and several large limousines preceded the royal car itself which was fitted with tinted glass and gave the occupants an almost fairy story-like appearance. The royal waves of the hand were bestowed upon us.

As the royal car approached the order came, 'Caps off, and three cheers for their majesties!' All of my republican sentiments rose within me, and my dislike of the hereditary system of rule burnt fiercely. But my protest had to be a silent one. I waved my cap in as near an imitation of the royal wave as I dared and my cheering would have registered zero on any decibel-recording machine. It all seemed to me to be a terrible waste of time and petrol.

But in the evening spirits were lifted when the local cinema showed the film *Thank Your Lucky Stars*. This was a film in which a bevy of Hollywood stars did not merely have walk-on parts but, in a departure from their normal types of roles, sang and danced. It was strange to see such dramatic actors as George Tobias, Ida Lupino, and Olivia De Haviland jitter-bugging and generally playing the fool. I went to see the film two or three times, and in post-war years I chased it around wherever it was showing.

About a week after the royal visit we marched the same route to enact the same procedures for the Prime Minister, who was visiting the north. When his car drew near Churchill debussed and walked along the line, speaking mainly to the few veterans among us who were wearing campaign medals. He then hurried into his car to the customary three cheers.

My own assessment of Churchill was, and remains, very mixed. On one hand I knew him to be an arch enemy of the trade union movement, the man who had tried to 'strangle Bolshevism at its birth', and that he was guilty of numerous bad political judgements. On the other hand he had rallied the nation in the summer of 1940, and in 1941 he had sunk his hatred of the Soviet Union, welcoming her as an ally when she was invaded by Germany. As we marched back to camp I realised that I had seen a man of great importance, even if any admiration I had for him had to be qualified.

As spring was sprung it was not long before things began to speed up and we knew that we would soon be on the move. Many of our weapons were updated and the personnel designated for the Scots battalions all headed south. Later in the year we met up with many of them, only to learn of the terrible rate of casualties they had sustained in the PBI (Poor Bloody Infantry).

We who remained had only a week or so before, in the third week of April, we too began our journey south to enjoy the sea breezes of Brighton; not for one of the dirty weekends for which the resort was infamous, but for dirty work of a very different character.

'Cuddle up a Little Closer'

In the spring of 1944, a popular song was 'Cuddle up a Little Closer Baby Mine', and the theme of German propaganda regarding the Second Front was similar in some ways to this melody. Yes, do come over; get close, and then we shall knock the shit out of you as we did during the Dieppe raid of 1942. But who would be doing most of the knocking was the question that lay heavily upon us in 1944.

My unit left Otley on Hitler's 55th birthday, 20 April, some seven weeks away from D-Day. We who had motored up north the previous year headed down south again, but in the seven months that our battalion had spent in Yorkshire, our character had changed and we were far more prepared for action than before.

The journey to Brighton was fairly uneventful and the weather was dry, which made a lot of difference to all DRs who were shepherding the convoy along. Fairly late in the evening on the second day, as we drove into the centre of the town, I remember seeing the sea before me and thinking that it looked a formidable obstacle to cross.

We then had to swing eastwards and come to rest at Kemptown, about a mile from Brighton proper, where a number of elegant empty houses in and around Sussex Square had been requisitioned for our use. Naturally it took several days for us to settle down and for a routine to be established.

During the spring of 1940, just before the War had turned nasty, I had cycled down to Brighton with a group of workmates. We had spent the night at a Youth Hostel in Patcham, just north of the town centre, and a good time was had by all. But now a different type of stay lay before me.

I did not know Brighton very well, but I was aware that many of its buildings and the famous Pavilion, a former royal palace, owed much of their elegance to the influence of the Prince

February 1940. The Author... Sweet sixteen and blissfully unaware of the firestorm that was soon to engulf Europe.

Summer 1940. 'Holidays at Home', a weekend at Henley-on-Thames. Next to me my ex-school friend John, who later won the Distinguished Flying Cross for his exploits over enemy Europe and, far left, work collegue Ted, who was killed on active service.

March 1942. A mugshot required for Home Guard identification purposes.

May 1942. As potential harbingers of bad news, we telegraph lads were dreaded by those who had relatives in the armed forces.

February 1943. Now Private 14405896, and Hitler begins to sleep a little more uneasily.

March 1943. A watchful group of warriors on standby one Saturday afternoon in Hounslow barracks, West London, and ready to spring into action if the need arose.

May 1944. With wartime comrade 'Jesse' James just before the long awaited D Day.

A post-war shot of one of the formidable fortifications that helped to cause carnage among US troops on the Omaha beach.

July 1974. Now able to stand on two legs and wondering exactly where I lost out to German mortars that fateful day almost exactly thirty years previously...

July 1961. Taken at a time when a revival of German militarism seemed a distinct possibility.

Regent, who later became George IV. The Prince was a gambler, drunkard, and womaniser, while remaining head of the Church of England. The philandering of the Prince with Mrs Fitzherbert and his many other mistresses no doubt helped to establish Brighton's reputation as a suitable place for nocturnal hanky-panky. Activities of this type flourished, particularly after the advent of the railways gave the so-called lower classes scope for a 'dirty weekend.'

Although we were in Brighton for a comparatively short time, much was packed into our stay. Hours were spent making all motorised vehicles waterproof and capable of affecting a landing, if it proved necessary for them to be dropped several yards from the shoreline. Motorbikes did not come into this category, so I spent a great deal of time on rough riding exercises and running messages. Some of these were to posts in beautiful parts of Sussex.

Another activity for DRs was to learn the potential dangers of the personal weapon with which we were issued, the Sten gun. This weapon was a cheap and nasty version of the Thompson light machine-gun (the Tommy gun), but the differences were marked. An important point was that the Sten had no safety catch, which meant that it was highly dangerous to leave a loaded magazine in the gun, for a sudden jolt could cause the spring controlling the firing mechanism to be jerked backwards and fire the weapon as it carried a bullet 'up the spout'.

With this danger in mind, all DRs, who from necessity had to wear the gun strapped over their shoulders, were warned not to ride around with the magazine in the firing position; a sudden jump from a bike could cause the spring to operate and endanger the rider. This warning was, unfortunately, all too frequently ignored. I remember the chief surgeon at the hospital where I later became a patient using strong language regarding the type of gun. While he was treating a Sten gun casualty, he exclaimed, 'Those bloody things, they have inflicted more damage to our personnel than they have to the Germans.' This claim may have been an exaggeration, but the point was clear to those who had experience of the 'bloody things'.

Several developments brought the front line closer. We were

informed what would happen if we were wounded. If this occurred, it was promised, one would be taken to a Field Aid Post (FAP), where one would be given a shot of morphine to deaden the pain, a cup of hot sweet tea to overcome the shock and a cigarette to calm the nerves. Such information was received with considerable scepticism. Hot tea and cigarettes were difficult enough items to obtain when on manoeuvres; was it likely that they would be available on the battlefield?

Another portent that battle was nigh was that we were invited to make out our wills. In this period, a will could only be legally binding if made by people aged 21 years or more, but there was an important exception to this age limit for personnel about to embark on active service. To help us would-be testators, we were supplied with an example will form, whose lines we might wish to follow. This read: 'I, Private Bloggs, hereby bequeath my estate to my next of kin, Mrs—'

As some struggled with such words as 'bequeath' and 'estate,' the concentrated silence was sometimes broken by the request, 'Hey Charlie, lend us a fag will you?' It was obvious that the liquid assets of some of the estates involved were slim indeed.

I bequeathed my estate to my mother, handed in the will form and forgot all about it. But, several weeks after I had been discharged from the army, I received a registered letter. I opened it with some excitement, hoping that it would contain a cheque for some back pay or some honorarium in recognition of my outstanding military service. Alas for my ego, neatly enclosed in the envelope was my last will and testament. As my estate had scarcely increased in value, I did not think that a re-write was necessary.

Another sign of the coming conflict was that we all had to send various items of clothing and any bulky personal effects to our home. Boxes were provided and all postage was paid. Later, I learnt that when my box arrived my father was quite upset. Being an ex-soldier, he realised the significance of its arrival.

Oh for a Dip in the Briny!

Stretches of the beach had been cleared of mines for the danger of invasion was now only a remote possibility. But bathing in the sea at Brighton at low tide has its disadvantages as the beach is one of pebbles and rocks. The nearby Black Rock swimming pool was more inviting.

The only trouble with the pool was that it had not been used for years and the water was, to put it mildly, turgid. It would easily have qualified for a place in the TV show, *A Life of Grime*. But we had only recently been inoculated against nearly every disease known to man. So what if the water were a trifle murky? We were obviously immune from all infections.

We jumped into the grim mixture, which felt like canteen jam – only the smell was different. Luckily, one of our sergeants came along and ordered us to leave the water immediately. Our pleas that we were immune from any malady were met with the deft, one-word reply of 'bollocks'. Thus was Brighton saved from a possible major outbreak of cholera.

As we prepared to reopen the western front, in the east the Red Army was sweeping forward. Most of the Crimea was liberated and a fierce battle for Sebastopol, the scene of an intense conflict in 1942, was raging.

Part of our preparations was to stage a demonstration for the brass hats. This involved our travelling to the countryside, where a long crawl over a never-ending field – with the necessary lugging of our machine-guns – was undertaken to show how an enemy position could be fired upon. A recording of our language might well have proven more daunting than any potential firepower.

There was one spot of relief in this task. On our way to the location, we had to pass the famous Roedean School for Girls. Rumour had it that on the walls of the dormitories were notices which read, 'Ring if you require a mistress.' Nobody knew whether this were true or not, but it was too good a story not to be believed. Hence, as we passed the school, there were always bawdy comments concerning for whom the bell should be tolled.

Then, early in May we were given twenty-four hour passes, distributed on a staggered basis. Mine began on a Friday and I was due back at 2359 hours on the Saturday. But Saturday evenings were the time for having a good time and my return did not take place until the Sunday. I knew I would not be able to talk my way out of the charge for being absent, and so I was given seven days' detention.

In the Nick

Detention in the army was not usually a pleasant experience. All barracks had their guardrooms, which housed short-term prisoners who would be given menial tasks such as scrubbing floors and peeling mountains of potatoes. They were escorted everywhere within the compound, so that it was clear to all that they had been naughty boys. In the evening between supper and lights-out, they were given rusty mess-tins to clean, only to see them dumped back in buckets of water to undo their work. Cigarettes were forbidden at all times.

Long-term prisoners with sentences over twenty-eight days faced a miserable ordeal at an army prison at Northallerton in Yorkshire. This 'Bleak House' establishment, commonly known as the Glass House, aimed to break the strongest of spirits. Even slopping out in the morning had to be done at the double. So I contemplated the next seven days with trepidation; would I crack under the strain? Actually, they proved to be one of the best weeks I had in the army.

We had no conventional guardroom, and we prisoners slept in rooms no different from our normal Sussex Square quarters, except that the doors were locked at night. By day we worked in the cookhouse under the supervision of the corporal cook, Tom Wolfenson, who was not only a good cook but a very decent man to boot. Once he was sure that we would not abscond, which would have involved him in lengthy enquiries, he treated us very well indeed.

He allocated us only necessary tasks – no rusty mess-tins – and spoke to us as human beings. We ate extremely well and altogether there was a pleasant atmosphere. Each morning I would ask him for permission to go round the corner where the vehicles were parked, so that I could check on my motorbike. Tom had to allocate somebody to escort me, and in a leisurely fashion we ambled along. But also round the corner was a newsagent and each morning my escort would stand outside while I went in to buy my *Daily Worker*.

Army regulations had to be obeyed, and these decreed that each man, when possible, should have at least one bath per week.

About halfway between Sussex Square and the town centre was a rather old-fashioned public baths, to which my unit had access. An escort called Jones was ordered to accompany me to the baths and watch like a hawk to ensure my safe return.

When my hawk-eyed escort and I arrived at the baths, Jones told me that he would wait outside, as he had taken the plunge only the day before. A bath a day was outside his reckoning. So I wallowed in the hot water and scrubbed parts of my anatomy that remained unscrubbed from one week to the next. I remained in the tub until I felt that if I stayed any longer my vigilant escort might think that I had escaped down the plughole.

I emerged from the gloom of the baths into the sunlight, where I could see nothing. Nor, after focus returned, could I see Jones, for the simple reason that he was not there. Cases abounded at this time of prisoners escaping from their escorts, but of course I had to be different and blaze the trail of the escort escaping from the prisoner.

Knowing of Jones's propensity to drink tea, I crossed the road to a working man's café – plenty of workmen, but no Jones. I was now becoming concerned, for if I returned without him he could be in trouble. Then I spotted a small public garden. There, sitting on a bench with two young women, was the ever-watchful Jones. When he saw me approaching, he hurried to greet me. In a stage whisper that could be heard at the end of Brighton pier, he told me, 'We're all right for tonight Richie; I've arranged to meet these two girls in town.' A look of accomplishment was writ large over his face.

'Jonesy,' I replied in a tone I usually reserved for young children, 'aren't you forgetting something?' He looked blank. 'I'm in the nick, remember!' He could not have looked more surprised had I pulled a fully-grown rabbit out of my forage cap.

What he said to the ladies I shall never know, but we marched back to the unit in stony silence. I am sure that he held me responsible for frustrating, if not a blossoming romance, at least a one-night stand.

About the time I had run into trouble, a comrade named Bell, always referred to as 'Dinger', took himself back to Otley and his girlfriend. There he stayed for about a week, before returning to face the music. I believe that Dinger received the same sort of punishment as myself, only somewhat longer. This move on Dinger's part proved to be wise, for a few weeks later he was killed in action. At least he had enjoyed a few of the delights of adult life before his early death.

The rest of the period of my detention passed without incident, and on Sunday, 28 May – my twentieth birthday – I was freed to resume my normal duties. As it was Sunday there were few people about, and so I took myself off home.

This proved to be a rather sad occasion, for I knew another quick trip would be unlikely before the balloon went up. None of my friends was on leave, but I was able to have a birthday drink with my mother, father, Aunt Frances, and Uncle Bill. We were all in a rather sombre mood. For one horrible moment, I thought that my aunt might offer me a cup of cocoa, as she did on that cold disastrous night the previous November that now seemed so long ago. Even my uncle, usually a great raconteur, was strangely subdued.

My birthday group wanted to see me off at the station, but I had always resisted station farewells. On this occasion my refusal was more firm than usual, for I am sure my emotions would have got the better of me.

On my return to Brighton, more indications that action was imminent ensued. We all had to hand in our palliases and learn to sleep on the floorboards. Then came the news that all the diplomatic bags of the foreign embassies were to be censored, which was a drastic move indeed.

One midnight, just as the new corns on our hips were beginning to settle on the floorboards, we were all awakened by the order, 'All outside, everybody in full marching order!' We had previously been warned to be ready to move at a moment's notice, so we stumbled to get our gear together and move off to the cookhouse where our company commander was to address us.

He told us that Allied troops had landed in France and had advanced several miles in land. Our job was to get over there as soon as possible and back up our forces. It was all very convincing. We were then ordered to go outside and stand by our vehicles, ready for a last minute inspection before moving off.

It was at this point that Private Smart-Arse whispered that the whole affair was just a rehearsal and we would all soon be returning to the delights of the floorboards. As usual, Private Smart-Arse was right.

'Well It's Started!'

These three words, uttered to us on Tuesday, 6 June 1944, by our platoon sergeant will always remain in my memory. The 'it' was an attack, which was possibly the largest armada of land, sea, and air forces ever mounted. While the news was lacking in detail, we were told that a landing had been achieved and a fierce struggle was now taking place to extend the toehold.

Naturally our unit buzzed with excitement, but by mid-afternoon we found that we were saying the same thing and a kind of anti-climax set in. As desperate battles were being fought, I went to the cinema with my friend 'Jesse' James. We saw a typical Hollywood extravaganza of beautiful women cavorting around some flimsy plot, but in the interval – to the strain of Beethoven's Fifth, as Jesse informed me – the latest Pathé newsreel brought the situation back to earth with 'shots from the front'. Actually, they were library films of naval guns being fired and soldiers charging unseen opponents. But they were enough to make Jesse and me realise that a grim time lay ahead.

For the rest of that week we stooged around, attending to last minute details whilst bemoaning the dreadfully cloudy weather. This, we knew, was hampering air cover. It was not an item of idle conversation, but a matter of life and death to those seeking to consolidate the beachhead positions. Would the weather improve by the time we arrived? We were soon to find out.

Normandy: The Crossing

Six days after D-Day, my unit left Brighton and began its journey to Tilbury docks. My services as a DR were not required and I travelled perched on top of a Bren gun carrier. As we passed through urban streets, the local kiddies gave us a cheer and many of us began to throw our loose change in return. But this had to cease when one or two youngsters came too close to the wheels of the vehicles. Many middle-aged women waved goodbye, but their handkerchiefs were often used to dry their tears. They realised better than we did that, for at least a number of us, the goodbyes were final.

On the journey, we stayed under canvas at two transit camps. Here it was thought necessary to mount a protective guard over the NAAFI girls, for war brings out the worst in people as well as the best.

Our leaving Brighton had almost coincided with the arrival of the V1, the famous 'doodle bug', or flying bomb, which began to fall on South-East England on 13 June. But we in transit did not know of this latest weapon of mass destruction, so at our second camp we cheered like mad when we saw a V1 nosedive to the ground. We thought that an enemy aeroplane had been shot down by the intense anti-aircraft fire that had preceded its descent. Then along came Private Smart-Arse to inform us of the nature of the missile. We did not realise that the people of South-East England were in for several months of terrifying bombardment until the V1 was basically mastered but quickly followed by the more dreadful V2 which continued to blast the south-east almost until the end of the War. (The last V2 fell on London on 27 March, 1945.)

Derby Day, 1944

The most famous race in the English flat racing season is the Derby. By tradition, this had always been run on a Wednesday, but owing to absenteeism, wartime demands for increased output decreed that it should be run on a Saturday. And so, as the crowds were forming on the Epsom downs, my unit was forming up to embark on the Liberty ship that was to take us to France. The date was 17 June, a date I shall never forget.

Not to be left out of the great day, we held a shilling (5p) sweep on the result of the race. But my interest ended when I failed even to draw a horse. Hopes of winning the jackpot were somewhat qualified, however, by the legend that those who were lucky gamblers on troop ships were those unlucky enough to be among the first killed when action began.

If one believed in omens, the signs were ominous, for the winner of the race was a horse called 'Ocean Swell'. Little did we know how tempestuous the sea which lay before us was to prove. An unseasonable storm, apart from making the crossing extremely unpleasant, was to upset the plans for the entire campaign by the subsequent delays in landing supplies and reinforcements, which were vitally necessary to extend the still precarious toehold that had been established.

As I marched up the gangway to get aboard, what thoughts went through my head? I would be lying if I were to claim how proud I was to be about to help France escape from Nazi tyranny. Instead, my concern was that, as it took four hours to cross to France in peacetime, it would probably take six in wartime. So would we get a meal during the crossing? Six days later we arrived in Normandy; 'Ocean Swell' had been with us with a vengeance.

We sailed from Tilbury late Saturday afternoon, but by Sunday evening we had only reached the end of Southend pier. Our Company Commander, Major Phillips, explained that the convoy was now assembled and we should be arriving in France on Tuesday morning. So we slunk back to our respective nests to wait for events to unfold.

Whenever I cross to France in post-war years, and as I sit in the comfort of the lounge of the ferry boat with plenty of food and drink readily available, my thoughts invariably turn to my first Channel crossing. I never cease to boggle that it now takes less than two hours to arrive. Indeed, use of the Channel Tunnel takes much less. How different it was in 1944!

The Liberty ships of the period, on one of which we had embarked, were mass-produced vessels – the brainchild of the American Henry Kaiser – that were turned out in large numbers to help compensate for the huge losses to shipping caused by U-boats. But their standards of comfort left much to be desired. Into the holds, and, it would seem, every nook and cranny, men established their individual sleeping space. There were one or two hammocks, but the proud possessors of these seemed only capable of falling out of them or sustaining severe cramps in the legs and stomachs.

And what of the mod cons? Whatever permanent loos there were on the ship were denied to us 'other ranks'. Chemical latrines were installed on the decks and, as the journey grew longer and longer, the level of human effluent rose higher and higher. To add to the joys of this mid-summer cruise, the storm was causing widespread seasickness. To cater for this contingency we were supplied with greaseproof bags ('bags vomit' in the parlance of army stores manuals) into which suffering men gave their all. After use, the problem remained of how to dispose of them.

Where we washed, or indeed if we washed at all, is something I cannot remember. Nor can I recall the smell that we must have created, though undoubtedly it was very powerful.

The Captain is Drunk

On Monday morning we were at sea, but in more senses than one. The ship was going up and down, the skies were grey, and everybody was ill. Had General Rommel caught sight of us, he would have thought that a German victory was assured. A comforting feature was the complete absence of enemy counter-measures. Whether or not this justified the absence of any lifeboat drill or other emergency evacuation measures is questionable. At no time can I remember receiving any guidance on what to do if the enemy were to strike. Although we had an overwhelming majority of armed force, a sudden attack by 'E' boats was no doubt possible. Despite the potential dangers, I can remember sleeping extremely well, but this was due to ignorance of what could have happened.

Tuesday morning arrived and the situation remained the

same. There was no sign of land, nor preliminary orders in anticipation of the move we had been warned about. The sea, if anything, looked more uninviting than ever, but nobody had told us that the artificial 'Mulberry Harbour' had been damaged and that the choppy seas were still making impossible the transfer of men and materials from ships into tank landing craft that could run right up on to the beaches.

With no information available, it was hardly surprising that rumours should begin to circulate. 'The Captain is drunk and does not know where he's going' was one of the first. Then came, 'The Captain is a Nazi agent and has kidnapped us all.' Perhaps slightly more creditable was, 'We're not going to France, we're going to the Far East to fight the Japanese.' Of course, all of these stories should have been laughed overboard, but as time went by and no land was in view, the question arose of just where we were going. I cannot recall one of our officers coming on deck to put us straight.

Gradually, men began to find their sea legs and appetites extinguished by the mountainous waves began their rebirth. What a gastronomic delight lay in store.

A method of feeding men on active service was to supply platoons with boxes, known as Compo boxes, which contained the rations for a given number of personnel for a day. The contents were basically tinned meats, tinned soups, powdered milk, tea, and the *piéce de résistance*, army biscuits. But the powers-that-be realised that such rations could become monotonous and so some variation was introduced. Hence, tins of corned beef alternated with spam, tins of carrots with peas, and plum jam with raspberry. The only consistent item was the biscuits: the cast-iron type mixed with concrete was available. If the Mulberry Harbour had been made out of them, I am sure it would have survived all storms. For many months after I had returned to England, it was a joy just to eat bread, albeit the wartime variety.

A novel feature of the soups was that the lid of the sealed tin contained a small chemical cap. To obtain a tin of hot soup, all one had to do was pierce the tin, apply a lighted cigarette end to the cap and in less than a minute hot soup was available. Why this innovation never caught on in peacetime puzzles me. I can only think that costs or health reasons are to blame.

To make it possible to identify the various contents of the Compos, the boxes were clearly marked with a letter, which could facilitate ringing the changes on the different tins. But on our ship, all the boxes bore the letter 'G'. This meant the very same unappetising fare was on offer every day. A disturbing fact was that one of our number had been an employee of Lyons tea shops, and he would carry on describing the wonderful meals that one could obtain at very reasonable prices before the days of rationing.

At long last came the signs that our journey was about to end. On Thursday, land came into view and we were warned to get ready to disembark the next day. This time it seemed that the information was to become a reality.

And so on Friday, 23 June, we hustled and bustled to transfer into the tank landing craft that were to take us ashore. There was no opposition and we had a dry landing. All the hours spent waterproofing the vehicles had been proven an unnecessary waste of effort. A gendarme riding his bicycle was the only indication that we were in a foreign country.

Naturally, I have often reflected on the horrible crossing we made, and I would not recommend it as an ideal package holiday. But I was aware at the time that many people had experienced far worse misfortunes at sea. The press had told of torpedoed seamen who had spent weeks in open boats, existing on rainwater and the minimum of food. Army biscuits would have been a real cordon bleu lunch. Did these men ever recover from their ordeals?

So what were my thoughts as I quit the ship? I cannot recall that I was hungry; no doubt concern about the unexpected was dulling my senses.

Playing for Keeps

When I arrived in Normandy, the vital task of consolidating the Allied positions had been accomplished. When I left in the middle of July, there remained some very bloody battles to be fought before the position was to change drastically. I suppose my period in the province might justly be described as setting the stage for the breakout into France proper. Few realised what a heavy price this would entail.

As far as my unit was concerned, we were no longer on manoeuvres when, at the end of an exercise, those who had been judged dead by some white-arm-banded umpire could rise and resume normal duties. Henceforth we were to play for high stakes: our lives and limbs.

Owing to the storm that had delayed our crossing, we had to move up to the front line very quickly in order to fit in with the overall plan for attack. But this was easier said than done. The whole of the Division was disembarking and the task of getting everybody in place with the necessary back-up facilities was formidable.

By the time we had moved to our first position behind the fighting zone it was late in the day. Somewhat optimistically, I bedded down for the night, only to be roused shortly afterwards by the platoon commander who needed me to drive him pillion-wise to a conference point. It was cloudy and pitch-black and we had one or two attempts to find the exact location. Finally, we arrived and I was ordered to wait while the lieutenant went up a narrow path to make contact.

So this was my introduction to France; sitting on a motorbike in the dark, completely isolated, and wondering who might be lurking in the undergrowth. I cannot say that I was scared – that was to come later – but for the first time there was no bustling around me, it was a peculiar feeling.

Then came the footsteps of the lieutenant returning, but suddenly he paused. My immediate thought was that he had seen something amiss. But no, there came the sound of a cork being removed from a hip flask and, when he reached me, there was a strong smell of whisky in the fresh night air. My main regret was that I was not offered a swig.

The next two days were spent in a whirl of moving locations, checking equipment and learning where we were; sleep was at a minimum. On Sunday we had a briefing from our lieutenant, who stated that the five original Allied invasion beaches had linked up and formed a bridgehead, which was too strongly held for the Germans to displace us. Unknown to our lieutenant was the fact that his statements were backed up by General Rommel, who noted in his diary on 10 June:

> Unit commanders ... report the enemy has complete control over the battle area and up to 100 km behind the front ... enemy armoured divisions carry on the battle at a range of up to 3,000 m with maximum expenditure of ammunition and splendidly supported by the enemy air force.[1]

At the same time, we were encouraged by the knowledge that Germany had been in general retreat since the Battle of Kursk in July 1943 and in every theatre – Italy, the North Atlantic, aerial bombing, and on the eastern front – one German disaster was following another. Rome had been liberated just before D-Day, and the V1 flying bomb was not seriously hampering the Allied build-up of supplies. Surely the Normandy campaign, now that the bridgehead was firm, should be a piece of cake?

But Rommel's diary entry did not convey the fact that the German army still possessed a formidable array of weapons. Its Tiger tanks were regarded as superior to the American Shermans, which, owing to their propensity to catch fire, were nicknamed 'Tommy cookers' by the enemy. Also, the Germans were feared for their 'Moaning Minnies' (mortars) and their rapid-firing light machine-guns, the Spandaus. How effectively were they to use these weapons and their other means of knocking shit out of the Allied troops?

---

[1] Reynolds, *Steel Inferno, 1st Panzer Corps in Normandy*, 1997, p84.

June 26th; Operation Epsom

The story of the Normandy battle has been told in detail several times and I make no attempt to outline the moves that transpired.[2] Indeed, it was only when I read some of the post-war accounts and visited Normandy some thirty years later (1974) that I began to understand what the overall strategy was. At the time, I was too busy keeping as low to the ground as possible and surviving from one moment to the next to have a precise idea of our movements.

Our unit was to go into action at 0800 hours and give support to the attacking Scots Battalions of the Division, which included the Argylls, the Seaforths, and Gordon Highlanders. We were to reach our start line by 0600 hours, which we did, but we were hardly encouraged by the heavy rain that soaked us through and caused our vehicles to churn the already sodden earth into minor seas of mud. The murky skies meant that no air cover was forthcoming, and behind the rows of infantry lining up to their starting positions were the stretcher-bearers. Altogether, a grim picture indeed.

We had been informed that the objective of the attack was to advance on the west side of Caen in a general encircling movement, cross the River Odon, and force the Germans to retreat to the east. But what we had not been told was that it was Montgomery's strategy to draw the German army on to us British while the US forces built up in the west. I don't think it would have helped us if we had known; on the contrary, it might well have made us envious of the Yanks, although we were unaware that they were to suffer heavy casualties before achieving their spectacular breakout in August.

The Epsom attack began with an intense creeping artillery barrage. For something like two hours, with off-shore warships making an important contribution through their heavy guns, shell after shell whistled over our heads with such intensity that the noise began to get on our nerves, let alone those of the enemy on the receiving end. As the barrage moved forward, so did we, just

---

[2] See, for example, Wilmot, *The Struggle for Europe, 1954*; Maule, *Caen 1944: the Brutal Battle*, 1980; Gilbert, *Second World War*, 1999, Chapters 38–41.

behind the infantry whom we were supporting. It was then that I received my first shock, which made my hair stand on end. Lying on the ground was a recently killed Jock, who was wearing the same type of uniform as myself. So this could happen to me! Here was proof positive that we were no longer playing games.

For the next two days, confusion reigned supreme. We advanced and were counterattacked, there were quiet moments, and there were times when all hell was let loose. Around me, Churchill and Sherman tanks were going up like torches, which made the vulnerability of my motorbike all too obvious. From the burning wrecks, a wounded tank crew member with at least some of his clothing on fire would sometimes escape. Always there was the unmistakable smell of burning flesh.

However realistic post-war films have been, the missing factor has been the smell of the battlefield, which was a cocktail of rotting bodies (human and cattle), cordite and burning debris. But there were other ingredients that gave the cocktail an extra kick. They included the fear of booby traps, snipers, minefields, and enemy aircraft.

On our side, we saw first-hand a number of devices, such as Churchill tanks with huge rolls of chains fitted to their front. As they moved forward, the chains flailed the earth with the aim of exploding any buried landmines. Then there were the flame-throwers, horrible deadly weapons, which were used when the enemy was in a concealed position.

Some people have argued that the Blitz of the main cities was just as grim for their citizens as for troops in the front line of battle. True, I was never injured in the London Blitz, nor was I trapped underneath a bombed building. Had I been, my comparison of the two fronts might be different. But during the Blitz, one knew that death and destruction were coming mainly from the skies, allowing of course for delayed action bombs and falling buildings, about which there was usually some warning. During the hours of daylight, one knew that one was comparatively safe. But at the front one never felt secure, for danger was ever-present. Even when one was sent to the rear for a rest, the retreating Germans had often left booby traps and poisoned cider barrels. Also, as we shall see, even so-called rest areas were liable to receive the odd shell or two.

Unlike the First World War, there was no determined front line in Normandy. Certain villages and towns could be in Allied hands, but the situation in the surrounding areas was fluid. Normandy had an abundance of thick hedgerows (the bocage) and lush cornfields, in which enemy tanks and dreaded snipers could hide so that, until the fighting moved much further forward, no place could be deemed safe.

I saw very little of the *Luftwaffe*, but on one occasion a German plane started to strafe our position and there was a hurried diving into what cover was available. Every unit had its comedian and ours was no exception. As the enemy plane was about to disappear into the distance, our platoon funny man picked up a Sten gun and, brandishing this limited range weapon above his head, called, 'Come back and shoot it out you coward!'

The enemy pilot must have had extraordinary powers of hearing, for no sooner was the challenge issued than the plane banked and came back with all guns firing. By some miracle nobody was hurt, nor serious damage done. But as we emerged from cover, the air became blue with the expletives directed at our comedian. He remained strangely quiet for several days afterwards.

After the initial period of rapid movements, my platoon became besieged in a farmyard outside a village named Colville. This village features quite prominently in accounts of the battle for Caen and, had the Germans dislodged us, the setback would have been serious. Whenever bullets and shrapnel were in clear evidence, the situation was usually described as one where there was 'plenty of shit flying around'. Colville was a location that clearly came under this description.

Before we reached the village, the hectic nature of our movements, combined with my night-time perambulations with the platoon commander, resulted in my having had very little sleep. So, during the dawn 'stand-to' after we had arrived at Colville, I could not keep my eyes open at this time when an attack was most likely. I was so exhausted that my immediate comrades had to prop me up in the slit trench to give the platoon commander the impression that I was watching for the attack which, luckily, never materialised.

It was at Colville that the capacity of the Tiger tank became all too clear. What mark of Tiger was ranged against us I do not know, but whatever the mark they were formidable. In peacetime I had often been amused by the comic song, 'Hold that Tiger, Where's that Tiger?' For some inexplicable reason, the song kept buzzing around my head. But, as we battled against a determined enemy who was launching vicious attacks with his Tiger tanks to the fore, neither the tune nor the words seemed at all funny. Henceforth, any reference to a Tiger augured a threatening situation. Luckily for the allies, the enemy did not have enough of them, nor sufficient supplies of petrol, to be decisive, but those that were in service were dangerous enough. The cry, 'There's a Tiger up the road' instilled fear in our minds similar, I imagine, to that of people in rural India who were often prey to the four-legged variety.

But fear does not win victories and one countermeasure to the Tiger was to equip the Shermans with a heavier calibre gun, the Firefly, whose shells could penetrate the Tiger's armour. But perhaps the greatest factors were the courage of the crews of the Shermans and Churchills who, despite the weaknesses of their own vehicles, pounded away at their adversaries seeking their vulnerable points, the Allied anti-tank gunners who stood their ground, and the sheer guts of infantry men. The latter, armed with a glorified catapult-type weapon called a PIAT (Platoon Infantry Anti-Tank), raised their heads above the slit trenches to take aim at the tracks of the Tigers and, in so doing, risked incurring the full wrath of the enemy's heavy machine-guns.

Although I never witnessed the active use of a PIAT, a member of my platoon – a chap called Edmonds – took aim at the tracks of a Tiger that was threatening our position. Luckily for all of us, a heavier anti-tank gun brought the monster to a halt before it fired. The enemy crew then baled out and were promptly taken prisoner. As they were marched across the field into the farmyard area, the regimental sergeant major of the Jock battalion gave the order for the men to double. One of the Germans had been wounded and I can still remember clearly the agony on his face as he dragged himself forward.

No sympathy at all was shown to the wounded crewman. Instead, cries of 'shoot the bastards' were heard. I do not know if any of the prisoners spoke English, but the tone must have made it clear that the message was hardly friendly. The criminal shooting of prisoners in the Normandy campaign has been researched and has revealed some deplorable incidents.[3] But I saw none, and my impression is that they were on a very different scale from the Russian and Atlantic fronts, where any ideas of the Geneva Convention went by the board.

There were other delights at Colville. It was here that I saw a young Scot overcome with battle fatigue. He could not stop crying that war was terrible and that he could not take it anymore. Luckily, battle fatigue, or shell-shock, was treated with much greater understanding than in the First World War; but US General Patton, who was notorious for slapping a stricken GI and accusing him of cowardice, was unaware of the change.

At Colville, I shared a slit trench with the platoon's first aid man, a chap called Greene. When the shells started coming over, we would get as low in our trench as possible, but, before we could get it dug to its required depth, we had to squat facing each other with our heads about a foot apart. Suddenly, a piece of shrapnel whistled through the narrow gap between us and hit the side with such force that we realised what a dangerous place we were in. Somebody then told us that, as this piece of shrapnel had obviously got our names on it, we should be safe from now on. I asked for a written guarantee to this effect, but unfortunately none was forthcoming.

Gradually, the German attacks began to subside and so, after what had seemed a never-ending period, we were relieved by a battalion of the Welch Regiment to go to the rear for a rest. We had been in the line for just six days, but they were such that few of us will ever forget them, for baptisms of fire have traumatic effects. And what had we achieved? Most of us would have replied Sweet Fanny Adams, but that was not the real answer. The Germans were facing the harsh reality that not only could they not displace us, but Allied forces were getting closer to taking the key town of Caen.

---

[3] Reynolds, *War Crimes*, Chapter 10.

Postscript

In 1974, I stood once more in the farmyard at Colville. It was a warm Sunday summer afternoon and the setting was idyllic. The only noise came from the clucking of a few chickens and the buzzing of insects; the contrast with the 1944 scenario could not have been more marked.

As I stood there, memories of the wartime episode came flooding back: the explosions, the cry for stretcher-bearers, the tingling fear of a near miss, even the odour of the cocktail of cordite and bodies.

I wondered what had happened to all the men. How many Germans had managed to extricate themselves and make their way home, only to face the defeat and devastation of their country? How many British soldiers had made it all the way to the victory parade still nearly a year away? And what was the price in physical and mental suffering?

'You're very quiet,' said my wife, who was with me. I could not answer; a piece of emotional shrapnel that had been whizzing round the farmyard for some thirty years had suddenly become wedged in my throat.

Rest and Tranquillity – hardly!

After our initial taste of combat, we travelled several miles to the rear and began to make ourselves at home in a group of abandoned farmhouses. There was a general feeling of relief that our platoon had got through the first round without a casualty, but uppermost in our minds was the stark realisation that this was only the first round.

To add to our immediate joys, we were ordered to queue up for lunch – always a pleasant duty – and then it happened! We had relaxed too soon, for suddenly there came the shriek of enemy shells and all thoughts of eating were cast aside as we dived for cover. Our run of nil casualties was over, for Lieutenant Flateau was hit and the storekeeper of another platoon was killed. Afterwards, the resumed lunch was far from a jolly occasion.

The next few days were spent catching up with sleep and gathering our thoughts. Letters were sent home and I can remember assuring my parents that I was having a quiet time quite free from combat. For security reasons all our letters were censored and, with this restriction in mind, I began an epistle to my old friend Roly. Military affairs were taboo, so I let fly with some of my reflections on the political situation during which I referred to the visits that King George VI and Prime Minister Churchill had paid to our battalion earlier in the year. My comments were hardly red white and blue, and our company commander, Major Phillips, ordered me to change my remarks. I thought then, and still do, that he was exceeding his authority, for the purpose of the censorship was to ensure military security, not political correctness. But, as I had enough battles on hand, I merely accepted his ruling.

Of course, stories were exchanged of what had happened in our individual areas, and we were all too aware of the missing faces. One platoon had suffered particularly badly. 'Dolly' Gray had been killed by friendly fire, several others by the enemy, and a number wounded sufficiently for them to be sent to the rear. None of us claimed that we had been brave; on the contrary, most of us referred to moments when we had been shit-scared.

My main job during the rest period was to follow the company commander around and carry messages to appropriate units. The fields on most sides of the roads had been laid with landmines, and skull and crossbone notices gave dire warning to this effect. Also, there were warnings that 'Dust means shells – Slow Down!' They all added to the pleasure of riding through the French countryside.

On one trip to another unit, the sky became filled with hundreds of Allied bombers whose target was the vital town of Caen. Rumblings in the distance signified that the bomb loads were taking their toll. All of this was very encouraging at the time, but when Caen fell on 9 July, the heavily rubble-filled streets proved impassable to important Allied vehicles. Numerous accounts have been written about the effects of the bombing and a hushed up contemporary report by Churchill's scientific advisor, Professor Solly Zuckerman claimed that the bombing had done little to hamper the capabilities of the German forces. This might be true, but the uplift it gave us was considerable, whilst the effects of the bombing upon German morale must have been devastating.

The days slipped by and, on the evening of Sunday, 9 July, we moved up to the front once more. If only they had kept those damned stretcher-bearers out of sight, one could have felt a little more at ease.

Evensong at Eterville

The position of the German army was now becoming desperate, but this was not obvious at the time even to the top brass, let alone to us who were too close to the trees to see the wood. Indeed, despite the plight of the Germans, post-war accounts reveal that at this time the Allies were becoming increasingly concerned at the slow rate of progress, and fears were expressed that the whole Normandy campaign was becoming bogged down in a war of attrition similar to the 1914 conflict.

On the local level, we did not know that, just before we had staggered into Eterville – a small town on the west side of Caen – Operation Charnwood had started a few days earlier (the 8th). This was a major offensive, which had the objective of taking the Carpiquet airfield. Our task was to follow up and help consolidate the gains that had been made. It was in the late morning of the 10th that my unit reached the southern part of Eterville.

Certainly, the enemy was doing all it could to displace us from Eterville. Parts of the town changed hands several times, but we in our area were not dislodged. This holding operation was not easy and our guns started firing immediately after we had arrived, as the counter-attacks came in.

The effectiveness of our guns earned the compliments of the officer in charge of the Jock battalions whom we were supporting, but it was known that German infantry had filtered through and had to be dealt with before they could do serious damage. Our platoon sergeant ordered several of us to follow him and so, clutching my near useless Sten gun, I went forth. Luckily nothing was found and it was with considerable relief that I returned to the comparative safety of our guns.

On the way back, I came across a dead German soldier. Nothing surprising about that, except for the fact that he was completely black and I knew that Hitler's racial policies forbade the use of black personnel. Apparently, it was common for the heat and explosives to bring about the blackening process. A feature of the episode that I remember all too well was that, at the end of the German's blackened nose, there crawled a very white maggot that was having the feast of its life. Such were some of the lovely sights of front line life.

Most of us disliked the uncertainties that the hours of darkness brought, and this particular evening was to prove a nightmare. As the sun set, the enemy tanks attacked and all hell was let loose. A certain amount of panic was in evidence and, much to his credit, Lieutenant Chamberlain, commander of a fellow platoon, stood upon a Bren gun carrier and assured us that there were sufficient British tanks in front to deal with the situation. No sooner had he climbed down than a rain of mortar bombs came crashing down.

A fragment from one of these bombs hit an old comrade of mine in the arm. I had known Bob Simpson since we started our recruits training together at Chester, which now seemed an age ago. Bob was now classified as one of the walking wounded and, although his injury was not serious, he needed medical attention. So on to the back of my motorbike he climbed and I took him to a Field Aid Post (FAP), which was about a mile away.

The journey was extremely dodgy and I was not sorry when we reached our goal. I wished Bob luck, and I have not seen him since. I am sure his wound never killed him and I am unaware of whether or not he returned to the front. It was a feature of the War to bring people together, only to separate them for good.

I was now faced with a dilemma: how was I to get back to my unit? As I began to retrace the path I had taken earlier, the situation had become much more dangerous. Eterville was the centre of a gigantic fireworks display. Was I to sail into the fray in the same style as Errol Flynn, when he had led the *Charge of the Light Brigade*? I decided to delay until the position had cleared a little and I waited until morning with a Jock unit in a reserve position just outside of the town,

The next morning, as I approached my unit's position, it was clear that the overnight fighting had been savage. A very bemused corporal from another platoon could not even tell me where the different sections of the company were and he obviously did not know whether it was two o'clock or Thursday. Actually it was 8 a.m. and Tuesday, 11 July, 1944 – a date I was to have good cause to remember.

When I reported back to Platoon Sergeant Stockman, he looked exhausted and did not question my enforced absence. The reason for the scenario of disorder is made clear from an account of the activities.

> Around midnight a major counter-attack by Panzer-Grenadier Battalions was launched against the hills to the north of Maltot and Eterville respectively. The latter changed hands a number of times during the night and at dawn was held by the 9 Cameronians. At 0615 hours on the 11th the 2nd SS Panzer-Grenadier Battalion … recaptured most of Eterville. They lost it again by 1415 hours…[4]

The same author also stated that, 'at the end of one of the bloodiest battles of the Normandy campaign, the Allies had failed to eject the men of the Panzer Corps from the vital ground between the Odon and Orne'. And there was me cavorting around the area on a motorbike. My mum would have had a fit.

Almost the Last Post

In the early afternoon I was introduced to the new Platoon Commander, Lieutenant Robinson, who had arrived to replace the wounded Lieutenant Flateau. We pinpointed our position on a map and he then ordered me to take a message to Company HQ whose location he made clear. When I set off, the fighting had died down and I was getting to the stage where I was fed up with being frightened all the time. I was learning when to duck and dive.

I had not far to go to Company HQ, which I reached without incident. While I was awaiting a reply, I began chatting with Quarter Master Sergeant Frewin. The Quarter Master was the type of man who would have been at home in any business office setting and, although he was inclined to be fussy, he had a reputation for being efficient.

He also had a reputation for wearing his forage cap on the

---

[4] Ibid., pp.162 and 164.

exact centre of his head, instead of the customary rakish angle. We exchanged near-miss stories and he told me how scared he had been the night before when a high-powered shell had landed in a nearby field and he had felt the blast from it. I was on the point of asking him whether or not the shell had achieved the impossible and blown his cap to the side of his head when the company clerk called out that the reply was ready for me. If ever I meet Mr Frewin again, I shall put the delayed question to him.

Within a few minutes of leaving HQ, I crossed paths with an agitated fellow DR, 'Smudger' Smith, who called, 'Watch out, Richie, they're mortaring up the road!' Possibly this was part of the Germans' defensive action against the Allied attack referred to above. But I was becoming a bit cocky, so, after thanking Smith for the warning, I rode merrily on. Then, when I was only some 200 yards from the slit trench shelter at my unit's position, a rain of mortar bombs began their deadly descent.

The type of mortar the Germans were using fired salvos of six shells. These fell in a circular pattern and, when they exploded, the shrapnel from each whipped out at ground level. To be caught in the open was almost a certain death sentence. So, as soon as I heard the shells falling, I leapt from my motorbike and lay in the slight cam of the road seeking the maximum cover available.

At first the shells were falling at the furthest point from myself, but they quickly began their rapid circular movement towards me. I have never laid claim to bravery, so I was amazed how calm I was. 'Richards,' I said, 'you're going to get killed!'

As the explosions drew nearer, the customary shit was flying all over the place with a vengeance, and I was hugging that piece of Eterville ground with more fervour than I have ever hugged a woman. Sheer willpower was pushing me towards the Earth's centre. Surely the sixth shell had now been expended? But no, the final bomb of the salvo found a target: my right leg.

I had read and heard of wounded men who had lost limbs and not been aware of what had happened. All I can say is that this did not happen to me. The blow I felt was savage, like being hit by a blacksmith with a red-hot hammer.

My mind now went into overdrive. I knew only too well that I was bleeding and that bones must have been broken so that I could not move. I also realised that another salvo was likely to begin any minute and I could hardly rely on surviving another onslaught. So, with great presence of mind, I called for help. My lungs were unimpaired and I imagine that my shouts drowned out the rumblings of the artillery.

Luckily I had chosen one of the best places to be knocked about: almost exactly outside of a FAP. Within minutes two stretcher-bearers were attending to me, and they quickly moved me into the large house that was serving as the aid post.

Most of my lower clothing was then cut from me, revealing that my groin was awash with blood. For one awful moment a vision of a frustrated love life flashed before me, so I was greatly relieved when it was ascertained that the blood was emanating from two minor wounds I had sustained in my back.

After my damaged leg had been strapped to splints and some mopping-up had been performed, I was given the promised shot of morphine, a cup of hot sweet tea, and offered a cigarette which, much to the surprise of my carers, I refused after making some crack about tobacco stopping one from growing. (The connection between smoking and lung cancer had yet to be established.)

I was assured that I would be all right. 'Six weeks in hospital, then six weeks in convalescence, so you should be back with us just before Christmas,' prophesied one of the medical men. The idea of eating tinned Christmas pud and cold custard in some besieged foreign farmhouse was hardly appealing. Nine months later, I limped home from hospital.

The time was then ready for me to be moved but, before this was attempted, and as I did not wish my trip to Company HQ to have been totally in vain, I asked that the reply to the original message I had carried be taken over to my nearby unit. My carers also turned out the panniers of my motorbike and offered me the chance to take a few personal items.

So I began my return journey armed with my toothbrush, a fountain pen and, of all things, volume one of *Select Works of Karl Marx*. Stories abound of Christians in the First World War being saved from an enemy bullet by their bible covering their heart. My copy of Marx did no such thing for me, but one piece of shrapnel had cut the edges of one side of the book. I still have the volume in my possession and the account, which I wrote on the flyleaf a month later, serves as a poignant souvenir of that unforgettable day. Later I realised how stupid I had been to go charging into action against an army so hostile to Communist ideas with such a book in my possession. I shudder to think what would have happened if I had been taken prisoner. I am sure that the Geneva Convention would not have saved me.

With friendly words, I was placed in a field ambulance and told another casualty was about to come on board. The poor chap who was then loaded into the vehicle was an infantryman suffering from a severe bout of shell-shock. He was quivering so much that the whole ambulance shook and, when our nearby guns opened up, I thought the poor fellow would disintegrate. No words of assurance from the accompanying medical orderly could comfort him. We had to wait until several more salvoes of mortar had dropped, but at long last the ambulance lurched forward.

I have often thought of those brave personnel at the FAPs. Their work was of the highest standard and their task of picking up war-racked bodies, patching them up, and then dispatching them to comparative safety while they remained in the forefront of danger, surely merits outstanding commendation. In common with many men, I owe them a great deal for helping to save my life.

On reflection, I have realised that, if I had to sustain a major wound at all, I could not have been luckier. I had survived being caught out in mortar fire with no cover, the main piece of shrapnel from the offending shell had hit me in the leg – not in the back – and, had it entered at any different angle, it would have severed my leg. Also, I had been picked up quickly, so different from the many horror stories of men bleeding to death in agony and isolation.

At last the ambulance found its way to the field hospital; I was never to go on parade again.

Flat Out from France

My dive into the ditch on that fateful July day heralded a period of being flat on my back until November and not being able to stand on my two feet until March of the following year. If I had known the address of the Flat Earth Society, I would have applied for membership. My return journey to England came one step closer when I was taken from the ambulance and carried into the tented field hospital.

The smell of disinfectant and surgical spirit was overpowering and this was just as well, for I was aware that gangrene and germ infection at the front in the 1914 conflict had caused grievous loss of life and limbs. What I did not know was that the dangers of infection were known at least as early as the Crimean War of the mid-nineteenth century. I now understand that the hygiene measures undertaken by a sanitary engineer, Sir Robert Rawlinson, reduced the death rate in the infamous hospital at Scutari by half 'within a matter of weeks'. All power then to carbolic and the new wonder drug, penicillin. But the fight against germ infection in hospitals has still to be won.

As I lay in the field hospital waiting for attention, I could hear the German language being spoken. Yes, there were wounded prisoners present. Men who, a few hours earlier, were intent on knocking shit out of each other, were now united in the pain and suffering caused by the ever-increasing sophistication of modern weapons.

During the 1970s a TV programme called *MASH* was an amusing serial depicting life in a field hospital during the Korean War of the early fifties. The episodes concentrated on the antics of the doctors, nurses, and support staff; the patients hardly got a look-in. As a patient in a field hospital in 1944, I saw nothing amusing in the scenes that were being enacted before me. The results of playing rough were unfolding with a scenario of men's gaping wounds and missing limbs, accompanied by a cacophony of desperate moans and groans. To add to this was the rumble of distant guns, emphasising that war was still being waged.

I realised that I was not a priority patient; indeed, when I caught a glimpse of those being admitted, I began to feel something of a fraud. But then I was whipped off to the operating theatre. As I was going under the ether, a rather strange thing happened: the sight of the living room in the house where I lived when I was nine years old, when I had had my last surgical operation, came back with great clarity. No doubt there was some rumbling of the subconscious.

When I came round, my reaction to the ether was marked: I could not stop spewing. During the pauses between spewing, an acute thirst took over, so I drank a little water and the spewing process started once more. To think I had once laughed at the drunkard film star WC Fields's plight when he talked of 'the day I nearly drank a glass of water'. Now my idea of bliss was to quaff one glass of the stuff after another. To add to my discomfort, I began to receive regular injections of penicillin and other drugs, so it was not long before my arms began to resemble pin cushions. But gradually my feelings returned to a more normal state and I was deemed fit for the next stage of my journey. I have hazy memories of spending a night in an empty cottage, before being placed on a hospital ship.

The return journey was very different from the outward bound venture and took about six hours, compared to the previous six days. Meals were offered to the patients, but the thought of food made me want to retch. As I lay in the hospital bed, not making do on the deck as on the earlier occasion, I realised how vulnerable I would be if the ship were hit. I did not reckon my chances of survival as being high; an odds-on bet if ever there was one, but I cannot say that I worried very much.

Finally, in the late evening of Saturday, 15 July, I was transferred to a hospital train at Southampton. I had been out of England exactly four weeks, in which time I had experienced more than I ever wanted to do again in such a short space of time. On the hospital train, I realised that my brain was not working very well, for it took me about twenty minutes to see the point of a simple joke in a cartoon in an available magazine. But, by the time the train reached Basingstoke, I was able to think more clearly and at least understand that our destination was Park Prewett Hospital, the main hospital of the region.

A Medical Wash and Brush-up

No man can experience a blanket bath and retain his dignity, and I was no exception to this generalisation. On arrival, two very efficient nurses divided my body into sections and each duly scrubbed away until parts of my skin gradually surfaced. Then a great quantity of grime, diluted stale sweat, and my dignity went down the plughole. But all was not over, for there remained a week's growth of beard to be hacked off. This task was designated to a junior nurse, a young lady of some eighteen years, who had no idea of the purpose of shaving soap. She applied one or two dabs of the essential softening agency to my face and then started to hack away with a razor to ascertain just what handsome features were concealed under the stubble. Although I was feeling extremely weak, I used my remaining strength to take over the rest of the process and succeeded in preventing facial disfigurement being added to my list of injuries.

The next few days were spent having various examinations of my leg under anaesthetic, receiving regular penicillin injections, and recovering from the minor stomach upset which the trauma had caused. It was not until the Tuesday afternoon that I surfaced again and began to take notice. As I lay in my bed, on that peaceful sunny day, the War seemed miles away, until the distant wailing of an air raid siren brought reality a little closer. But nothing happened nearby, for most of the V1s were falling nearer to London. However, the sirens made me think of my parents; were they all right and surviving the dangers of London? By now they were probably beginning to worry about me.

At this point it might be helpful to reflect upon the poor state of communications in comparison with those of today. In common with most working class families of the period, my parents' house and that of our neighbours had no telephone. Indeed, my mother, like many others of her generation, fought shy of the phone for reasons that most modern-day youngsters would not comprehend.

So I decided to send a telegram. To this day, I am not sure where I got the money from to pay for the wire, but I can remember that I had to be brief. So I merely stated that I was back in England, was OK, and only knocked about a little. I promised to write in detail 'soon'. But I learned later that this brief communication did more harm than good and had my parents on tenterhooks wondering what had happened to me.

This little episode was to remind me of a story my Uncle Bill used to tell of his 1914 adventures. Apparently, under intense pressure in the trenches, he sent a field postcard to his wife, crossed out all the optional messages printed on it except 'I am well' and signed it 'Bill.' About a fortnight later he received a reply, 'So am I, Frances.' On reflection, I think that my telegram was about as useful as my uncle's postcard.

On the same day as my unhelpful telegram, a walking communication problem came into the ward in the shape of a chap called Walden, a member of my company. He spotted me and made his way over to my bed, displaying no sign of any physical injury. He quickly told me that the trauma of Eterville had rendered him speechless, literally. For several days he had been unable to utter a single word, but he had just been given a powerful shot in the arm that had put power back into his vocal chords. Whether or not he went back to the front I do not know, but I met him briefly by chance in central London just after the War, so I am aware that he survived.

I was now in much better shape than when I had arrived at Park Prewett and it was decided that I was ready for major surgery. So, on Thursday, 21 July, I was moved to Harlow Wood Orthopaedic Hospital near Mansfield, which is close to the city of Nottingham. The date is easy for me to remember, for on the previous day the July plot on Hitler's life had been attempted. I learnt of the plot from one of the medical orderlies in the ambulance on the journey north.

Much has been written about the July plot, the perpetrators, and the brutal treatment they received after their failure. What might have happened had Hitler been killed is, of course, one of the big 'ifs' of history. But it seems highly doubtful that Germany would have fought to the bitter end as it did had Hitler's death allowed the Nazi hierarchy to disintegrate into bitter rivalry.

Harlow Wood – not Tinsel Town

It was easy to confuse the spoken 'Harlow Wood' with the movie centre 'Hollywood', but there all similarities ended. There was nothing fictitious about Harlow Wood; no romantic Doctor Kildares walked the wards, nor were there heroes with convenient flesh wounds lying around to arouse sympathy. There was only the stark reality of treating men whose initial injuries had been sufficiently cleaned so that the surgeons could see the bones from the flesh. When the necessary surgery had been completed, patients would then be farmed out to lesser establishments to allow scars to strengthen and bones to knit.

During the first evening in my new destination, the ward enjoyed a visit from a small group of hospital volunteers. Such people gave up their time and incurred all sorts of expenses in performing tasks that patients could not do for themselves and the hospital staff had no time to undertake. It was really kind of such people to go to the troubles they did, and their services and friendly approach were of great help.

A lady of some forty years came to my bedside and asked me if she could bring me anything from the town shops or write any letters for me. The good lady then wrote to my parents, giving my latest address and assuring them that I was basically OK.

The following day, my treatment began in earnest. I have the notes on my medical progress at Harlow Wood, which were supplied after the War when I was in dispute with the Ministry of Pensions. These show that an operation took place shortly after my arrival at the hospital to align the fractured tibia and to remove foreign bodies. What I find particularly interesting is the statement, 'Pus escaped on removing packs. Swab taken.' Hence, despite the penicillin and other drugs that I had been given, my leg was infected and further measures were necessary to solve the problem. This indicates how, under different circumstances, amputation would have been highly probable. What happened to me is some indication of how the comparatively new drugs must have saved thousands of limbs.

For two days after the operation I suffered intense pain and was taken down again to have my leg examined by Mr Parker, the senior surgeon who had set my leg.

I was, of course, not the only one to be suffering and a steady level of groans filled the air of the ward. Suddenly, a man who was my near namesake raised his head and cried, 'Oh God, why do I have to suffer such pain? Take it away and share it out among the others!' For some reason his appeal to the Almighty was not supported by those designated for a little more suffering. Sick as fellow patients were, a few explicit responses opposed the suggested re-allocation.

On the third day after my operation, the wounds began to settle down and life became reasonably pleasant. Then, with incredible timing, my mother, having received news of my address, walked into the ward. The look on her face told the story of acute anxiety concerning the state in which she was going to find me, and whether or not I had made light of my injuries.

A nurse directed her to my bedside and for at least a minute neither of us could speak. Then the floodgates of our exchanges began. How was I? Would I recover completely? Would I be coming home? In turn, I wanted to know how my parents were and whether they had news of my brother, who was in the Italian campaign. What was the latest on the V1 offensive and had London been severely damaged?

After these and other exchanges, a hospital volunteer arranged overnight lodgings for my mother. She explained to me that she wanted to return home the next day, as my father, who was not in the best of health, would be anxious to know the news. She was obviously relieved to have learnt that my injuries were not too bad. So, after a tender farewell, she left promising that she and my dad would come again soon.

Hardly had my mother got through the door, when the results of a swab taking came through and I was placed on a penicillin drip. A huge needle, which felt that it was the smaller sister of the type associated with Cleopatra, was inserted into the thigh of my sound leg, and an overhead bottle began to feed its contents into me. A very unpleasant four days began.

The treatment had both short and long-term consequences. In the short term, after the needle had been removed I could not move my good leg for some days, so now I had two bad legs, not one. In the long term, the collective amounts of penicillin that I had been given rendered me allergic to it for the rest of my life. But the main objective of defeating infection had been achieved.

It was about this time that I became aware of the antics of 'Nurse Nasty'. I always had, and still have, a marked respect for the skills and dedication of members of the medical profession. But there are always exceptions that prove the rule.

Nurse Nasty seemed to get some satisfaction in luring patients into a relaxed mood, only to turn on them in a most spiteful fashion. The general pattern would start with her asking me how I was and then chatting about my progress. However, a chance remark by me, or a request for some service, would be rewarded with a vicious response. Did I not know that there was a shortage of whatever it was that I was asking for and that there were more severe cases present who had clear priority over me? Why was I making such a fuss, when other patients were in a much worse condition than myself?

But I was only too aware of the plight of many fellow patients and I had never ceased telling myself that I had been comparatively lucky. Therefore, I found Nurse Nasty's remarks particularly unfair and hurtful. Later, the process would begin again; friendly remarks and smiles until I thought that the previous occasion had been a blip caused, no doubt, by the long hours that nurses were working. My guard was lowered, only for some piece of bile to be my reward. After being fooled about three times, I kept my guard up at all time and was glad when Nurse Nasty was off duty.

Why she acted in this way, I have no idea. No doubt there were some deep-seated psychological reasons. But the mental damage that she did to sensitive patients possibly offset the good work she did in helping them to recover physically. Luckily, the Nurse Nasties are rare, for I never encountered another one in the remainder of my hospital sojourn.

Meanwhile, back in France

It was now early August and I began to take an interest in what had been going on since I had left my comrades to their fate. Shortly after I had been KO'ed, General Montgomery had unleashed Operation Goodwood. This was a massive offensive launched on the east side of Caen, with the objective of achieving substantial results. It was regarded as a failure in relation to making a decisive breakthrough, but a long-term assessment was that it helped to use up the German armour at a vital stage of the campaign.

Even with the British engaging much of the German armour, the Americans had come under extreme pressure at Mortain to the west of Normandy, where the German army sought to drive through the Allied-held territory, reach the coast and split the Allied forces in two. It was an impracticable plan devised by Hitler, as the Germans just did not have sufficient men or materials to carry out its objectives. The hastily assembled German forces and their drive to the coast put them in serious danger of entrapment. But no German general was in a position to oppose Hitler, for after the July plot it was easy to be accused of treason.

The daily papers did not convey the full story of the campaign and behind the headlines, which over-praised every Allied advance, there was a feeling that things were going slowly – too slowly. But there were positive things to report and from the safety of my hospital bed I read that huge numbers of the V1 buzz bombs were being destroyed on their way to London, either by anti-aircraft fire, or our fighter planes. Apparently, Spitfire pilots were flying alongside the V1s and using their wings to tip the robot bombs off balance. The V1s would then crash to the ground, hopefully in remote areas.

What was also noticeable from the papers was a cooling of relations with Soviet Russia. The Western governments were becoming apprehensive of an excessively powerful Russia arriving at the Peace Conference now looming on the horizon. If the Red Army could defeat the *Wehrmacht* in the east, as it was doing, would this not create a strong post-war Soviet Empire in eastern Europe?

These suspicions were deepened by the events surrounding the Warsaw uprising that had begun in early August, when Polish citizens rose against the occupying German forces without any prior consultation with the Soviet government. The poor relationship between Moscow and the London-based Polish government did not help when the uprising soon ran into trouble. The German army's response was savage and, despite the common enemy involved, there was a complete lack of Soviet support for the Poles, who continued to fight tenaciously. Although the Red Army was close enough to the capital to at least drop some much needed supplies, Stalin adamantly refused to offer any help whatsoever.

As a British Communist, I was concerned at the accusations that were being levelled against the Soviet Union, but I believed that there must have been good reasons for its lack of support for the Poles. If only members of the British Communist Party had known the real character of Comrade Stalin! But the simple fact was that the majority did not; only a few knew the true story. Consequently, when Polish issues and other questionable events surfaced in the post-1956 period after Kruschev had denounced Stalin, the effects on the British Party were devastating.

But to return from eastern Europe and the future, in August both of my parents came to see me. Throughout the War, my father had always been an optimist. According to him, Germany had been running out of fuel ever since the British army was kicked out of Dunkirk and, in any case, the Empire would ultimately ensure the victory of the mother country. Naturally, he was highly delighted with the failing V1 offensive and thought that London would henceforth be fairly safe. As with so many of his predictions, events proved him wrong. Less than four weeks later, the deadly V2 rockets began to drop on the capital, which raised the spectre of the need for a complete evacuation of London.

As an ex-professional soldier (1907-1919) my father had numerous questions concerning the weapons used in the Normandy campaign. I told him that, as far as I could understand matters, there were no great differences between the British rifles and machine-guns used in his war and those of the present conflict. But there were marked differences in the types of tanks, aircraft, and means of radio communication.

Our comparison of weapons was interrupted by a nurse tending to the patient in the next bed. My father asked me what was wrong with him and I replied that the poor chap had lost both his legs. I could see that my dad was quite stunned at the prospect of this young man being so disabled for the rest of his life. From our earlier discussion, it was clear that, although the weapons of the two wars had changed, there was consistency in the types of human suffering involved.

My parents' weekend visit came rapidly to an end and they left me feeling that, on the whole, things were not going too badly. It certainly seemed that way, and, as a sign of my personal progress, I was told shortly after their departure that I was about to be transferred to one of the subsidiary hospitals for the healing process to continue.

Wonderful Worksop!

Nearly every day in the month of August brought news of Allied military achievements, and the 15th was no exception. On that day in 1944, the invasion of southern France – Operation Dragoon – was launched, which helped to force the rapid withdrawal of the German army from the whole of the country. On the same day, I was transferred to the Kilton Hill Hospital in the Nottinghamshire town of Worksop. For the next eight months this was to be my base until, with a calliper on my leg and walking with the aid of a stick, I was to return home to resume life as a civilian. In this period, I watched the war in Europe drag on almost to its bitter end, while I had to adjust to my changing physical condition and pending civvy street status.

The hospital at Worksop was a fairly old building, but modern annexes had been added and it was one of these annexes, Ward Two, which I entered that August afternoon. There were about twenty-five beds in the ward and the first thing I noticed was how quiet it was; nobody seemed to be around. The reason for this was that most of the 'up' patients had made their way into town and were enjoying its delights. So, as I lay in my corner in almost splendid isolation, I began listening to Spike Jones and his City Slickers blaring out on the ward wireless the then revolutionary novelty number 'Cocktails for Two'.

I was to find the communal wireless a mixed blessing. Certainly it was an advantage to keep abreast of the rapidly changing news. Also, there was a wide variety of entertaining programmes such as *The Jack Benny Show* and *ITMA* (*It's that Man Again*), while a number of the big bands kept one up to date with numbers such as 'I'll Get By' and Judy Garland's 'Trolley Song'. But there were times when one disliked a programme or just wanted to be quiet. I was given the option of being moved out of earshot of the set, but this was going from one extreme to another, and could I turn my back on Judy Garland? If only transistor radios had been available!

When I arrived at Worksop I was a bed patient and for several months I was unable to visit the town. At this time, Worksop had a population of about 15,000 and the main male occupations were mining and light engineering. I was to find that the town centre was similar to many others, having a main street, shops, two cinemas and a liberal number of pubs. But the people were special insofar as they were extremely kind to us patients. They helped us with our mobility problems and were extremely generous in all sorts of ways.

As the evening of my first day progressed, the flow of returning patients began and for the next few days most of my time was spent getting to know their names, as well as those of nurses, doctors and support staff. There was a fairly relaxed atmosphere, but I realised that there were at least some rules – and what would happen if they were broken.

The comparison with discipline in barracks was marked – for Worksop was a civilian hospital where there were no Military Police, nor machinery for handing out humiliating punishments such as jankers – yet the standards of behaviour were good. So how was discipline maintained? First, most of us patients wanted to recover, if not too quickly at least eventually, and ingrained in most of us was respect for the skills and knowledge of the nurses and doctors. Then there was the realisation that the military authorities were not far away and any offence could result in a loss of pay or transfer to a strict military hospital, where one got well by parade drill numbers.

Helping to maintain good order in the ward was the personality of Sister Burke, whose charm would bring any malcontent into line. She enforced the rules of the hospital in a liberal and sensible fashion, which we patients accepted as being in the best interests of everybody.

Immediately above Sister Burke in the order of authority was the matron, a mature lady whose status obviated the need for her to have any surname; a forename for Matron was also unthinkable. As far as we patients were concerned, Matron had two functions. One was to strike terror into the hearts of the nursing staff, the other was to sweep through the wards on a daily basis, giving the odd patient a frosty smile of greeting. No doubt these comments are a very unfair assessment of a capable administrator, so what a pity that matrons in general were often seen in such an unfavourable light.

Time on our Hands

The business of getting broken bones to heal is time-consuming, and filling in the hours while nature does its work can present its problems. As might be expected, my fellow patients were a mixed bunch whose main leisure activities involved telling jokes of a dubious quality, reading, and playing games. But, to help those with no imagination, an occupational therapist – a young lady in her early thirties – entered the scene.

She suggested that leather work was a practicable possibility and that there was currently a keen demand for ladies' handbags. Our therapist explained that she could obtain the necessary leather skins, linings, and other bits and pieces, as well as providing the essential tools. For an outlay of about a pound, a patient could apply his labour power and produce a bag that could realise between £5 and £6. This was a fair sum of money in those days, being roughly a working man's weekly wage.

So, for a few weeks until the fever abated, the ward was like a factory. Up patients were called on to do the required cutting out and bed patients were busy punching holes and thronging the respective parts together. Females from far and wide, young and old, began to be attracted to the ward in order to pick up a bag of their choice.

During my time at school, my three years of woodwork classes had produced a simple breadboard, which was hardly evidence of a practicable aptitude. Consequently, I had no desire to punch holes in my bed sheets instead of the leather, nor to produce a bag more suitable for heavy tools rather than feminine requirements. Instead, I began a correspondence course in maths and English, as well as getting down to some serious reading.

My motivation was twofold. First, I realised that my return to civilian life and work in the Post Office could not be far away and that any progress in my career in this area depended on passing a number of Civil Service examinations. Secondly, my interest in politics necessitated a much better grasp of basic subjects if I were to understand the complexities of economics and philosophy.

In these matters I was helped considerably by a sergeant major from the Army Education Corps. This comparatively elderly gentleman, a school teacher in civilian life, visited the ward on a regular basis to run debates, organise educational quizzes, give advice on careers and discuss lines of study with anybody who was interested.

He was most encouraging to my efforts and he kindly obtained various books for me from the local library. It was he who first put the idea into my head of taking up teaching, an idea that was to alter my post-war life. I owe him a great deal for his wisdom and patience.

There was always some turnover of patients and into the bed next to mine arrived a wounded Italian prisoner of war, who was immediately named Tony. Unfortunately, Tony could speak no English and nobody could speak Italian, which made communication a little difficult. But Tony could speak French and I had studied French at school, all of which I had promptly forgotten on starting work. So here was an additional challenge: to learn sufficient French to converse with Tony. How I began to massacre that lovely language I shudder to think, but at least some exchanges became possible.

Plastered!

When I had left Harlow Wood hospital my damaged right leg was encased in a massive plaster cast reaching from my toes to the top of my thigh. Its weight had been increased by the need for the plaster to be opened near the wound area in order that treatment could be administered, which meant that even more plaster had been applied.

By the time I arrived at Worksop, the cast was already several weeks old and beneath the plaster blood was gently oozing from my wounds. This, I was assured, was nothing to worry about, but shortly afterwards I did have a worry; namely, the smell of stale blood. As the weeks went by the smell increased and, aided by a few natural body odours, the nearby flowers began to wilt whenever the bedcovers were raised.

Apart from bedmaking, there were other occasions when the

covers had to be lifted, and one of these was when the physical training sergeant did his rounds. It was his job to encourage patients to exercise their damaged bodies as best possible and thereby help prevent limbs from seizing up.

PE instructors, who were generally referred to as 'Muscles', were an extremely unpopular sort for they seemed to take delight in subjecting men to bullying comments as they inflicted sessions of muscular torture on them. But things were different in the hospital scenario where there was no bullying and it was accepted that it was in our interests to make an effort.

When the sergeant first saw me, he asked if I could raise my sound left leg – no trouble. Then he asked if I could raise my damaged right leg, including its ton of plaster. I laughed and thought he was joking. But he persisted and told me he would help me to raise the limb, and he took hold of the bottom of the heel accordingly. I warned him that he was in danger of giving himself a hernia, but he raised the leg to an angle of about forty-five degrees and told me to try to control its descent.

I had always been proud of being reasonably fit, and mat work in the gym had been an important part of a workout, so I regarded the independent raising of my leg as a challenge. Within a few days I achieved my objective, much to the delight of the sergeant, who had me demonstrating the exercise to the other patients. Apart from feeling rather pleased with myself, I realised how important it was to try to keep limbs moving, and I am sure that I gained enormously from the exercises when I was at last able to get out of bed.

But problems with my plaster persisted. Beneath it, skin began to die and this caused an irresistible desire to scratch. My fingers would be inserted into the top of the plaster and temporary relief would be obtained; but not for long. As the fingers ran out of effective length, other objects such as pencils and toothbrush handles would be used as tools for excavation.

Every unit has its extremists and our ward was no exception. One patient, Jones, who was being driven mad by his itching, decided on something more drastic than the use of pencils and brush handles. Before each meal, all bed patients were supplied with the necessary cutlery. So what could be more effective in sharpness and length than a table knife? Hence Jones began his dead skin removal with gusto! But the law of scratching prevailed and new areas of skin soon craved attention. As these areas increased, Jones's grip on the handle of his knife was reduced to it being held at the extreme end of the handle by a finger and thumb.

And then, of course, the inevitable happened! His precarious hold slipped and Jones was left knifeless for lunch. To replace his knife was a simple matter, but what was to happen after the meal? How was the errant table knife to be retrieved? That was a question that concerned us all, for there we were, itching but, at that moment, not daring to scratch.

Immediately after lunch, a group of up patients drew the screens around Jones's bed and began to tackle the problem with zeal. Jones was almost stood upon his head and the shaking that ensued might well have displaced his lunch as well as the reluctant table knife. It was while Jones was giving this amazing display of involuntary gymnastics, that a frilly hat suddenly appeared over the top of the screens. Matron had appeared like the evil fairy godmother in a pantomime, who had suddenly arrived via the stage trapdoor.

Poor Jones was restored to a horizontal position with such a lack of ceremony that his other leg was in danger of being fractured in the process. In somewhat icy tones, Matron demanded to know what was going on. In reply, our highly embarrassed Jones weakly stammered that his dinner knife had fallen down his plaster. Somewhat naturally, Matron was surprised and asked how this could have occurred. 'Well, Matron,' said Jones with an incredible presence of mind that should have ensured his immediate promotion and transfer to the Intelligence Corps, 'I was eating my dinner, but the piece of meat was tough and I had to press hard on the knife, and it slipped from my hand and shot straight down my plaster.' Even Matron had to smile at this ingenious reply.

I have often mused on how Jones's hospital notes must have read. An entry such as 'plaster opened to remove table knife', would surely have come as a surprise to any medic not aware of the background of the errant piece of cutlery.

What about the War?

By the time I had reached Worksop, I began to receive letters from friends in my old company, even though they were written when the Allies were still bogged down in the boscage of Normandy. They referred to the slow progress being made and the casualties, particularly from German snipers. Several asked in anguished terms how long the carnage was to continue. Then the highly-charged radio bulletins and newspaper reports took prominence as the War sped up.

The progress of the Allied campaign in France has been well-documented and I seek only to mention how we in hospital followed the flow of events. For obvious reasons the news reports were, to use a modern political expression, highly spun, and gave the most favourable impressions possible. No mention was made of the inter-Allied rivalries that existed among the generals, which only surfaced after the War. Naturally, the newspapers made exciting reading, while wireless bulletins tended to run ahead of themselves. Newscasters sometimes had to correct their accounts of what had happened, and we cheered the news that Paris had been liberated at least three times.

Following the second D-Day on 15 August, the German position in France and elsewhere seemed to be collapsing and, in recognition of his part in the victories, General Montgomery was promoted to Field Marshal. The lightning advances of General Patton, the breakout from Caen, the slaughter of German divisions in the Falaise Gap, the momentous liberation of Paris, and developments in the Balkans, gave rise to a belief that victory in Europe could not be far away.

But, in September, the euphoria of August vanished. On the 8th, a reported explosion of a gas main was in fact the first of the deadly V2 rockets to land on London. This terrible weapon was so fast that it would land without warning and it was only afterwards that nearby residents would hear the noise of its descent. As many of us patients were Londoners we were concerned for our families, but what could we do? Worry was confined to the backs of our minds, for there would have been no point in our having long faces and biting our fingernails all day.

Then on the Sunday morning of the 17th, there began Operation 'Market Garden', the Arnhem adventure. After the German headlong retreat from France, it seemed inconceivable that the *Wehrmacht* could be capable of organising any major defensive action. Well after the War's end, I spoke to a Dutch citizen who, as a young man, had witnessed the shattered German divisions arriving in Holland from France, giving the impression of being a spent force. No doubt at that time Allied Intelligence had its spies making similar observations. How wrong appearances can be!

At first, 'Market Garden' seemed to be going well and glowing reports of the size of the attacking Allied forces were given. And then everything started to go wrong and I remember clearly the worries expressed by Night-Sister Fisher, when she sought our opinions on how the campaign was faring. Despite Montgomery's reputation for caution and meticulous planning, the operation ended in defeat, summed up by the title of the post-war film, *A Bridge Too Far*.

To add to the gloom of the war news, in the east the Warsaw uprising was dragging to a bloody defeat, which did not finally end until the October. Hitler then instructed his infamous henchman Himmler to wreak terrible vengeance upon the Polish survivors. At the time, none of us appreciated how the history of the uprising would cloud post-war international relations.

As September drew to a close and the hours of daylight started getting shorter, I realised that the men in my old company had been living in holes in the ground under dangerous conditions for some four months. And those months were in the summer. Now a bleak winter faced them, and my mind turned to our manoeuvres on the Yorkshire moors at the beginning of the year and all the discomforts involved when temperatures were freezing. What a pity that bomb had failed to kill Hitler.

Mr Parker is in Ward One!

In Richard Gordon's *Doctor in the House*, there is a hilarious account of what happened when the head surgeon of the hospital was about to do his rounds. Nurses dashed about like scalded cats, 'tidying the patients', who were then tucked in so tightly that a little shallow breathing was their only possible activity. His description of the scene reminded me of Saturday mornings in

Ward Two at Worksop, when Mr Parker did his weekly tour.

As soon as it was known that Mr Parker had arrived in the adjacent ward, things reached a crescendo. A great deal of ramming patients' belongings into lockers ensued, and bed patients were expected to have synchronised their bodily demands for bottles and bedpans before the great man's visit. To request either item when Mr Parker was in the ward was to enlist for involuntary euthanasia.

In my opinion, Mr Parker was a gentleman in the best sense of that word and was above all this mad scramble. On one occasion, he entered the ward and questioned why all the up patients were standing by their beds. It was explained to him that it was the customary practice that when an officer entered a barrack room all ranks would stand, and this practice prevailed in other venues. At this, Mr Parker gave a little groan and asked the men to sit down. 'If I want you to stand I'll ask when I reach you,' he wearily exclaimed.

Mr Parker had a reputation as a competent surgeon. He spoke to us patients in a sympathetic fashion and gave understandable explanations to our queries. The significance of one of his explanations was a little too easy to grasp, for when he told one patient that he wanted him transferred back to Harlow Wood for an operation, the patient asked why it could not be done at Worksop. Mr Parker replied that the surgical saws were both much finer and faster in the operating theatre at Harlow Wood. The poor patient turned a deadly shade of pale.

As the weeks went by, I lived in hope that my huge plaster would be removed for something lighter and less smelly, which could make a visit to the loo a possibility. While various aspirants to European kingdoms wanted to sit upon royal thrones, my much more limited ambition was to mount the type designed in the mid-nineteenth century by Thomas Crapper, whose revolutionary water closet led to the first half of his surname becoming synonymous with a call of nature.

At last, in early November, action was promised for the following week. My plaster was to be shed and my foot, which had become rigid, was to be manipulated under anaesthetic. Came the great day and two up patients pushed my trolley down to the theatre, where my half ton of plaster was discarded. It might possibly have been used as an essential part of the foundations of some new building project, but for the danger of giving rise to a belief that there was something wrong with its drains.

In the theatre I was given a light knockout drop of something, while Mr Parker examined my leg and took hold of my foot for its manipulation. According to my trolley pushers who were allowed to watch, a loud crack rang out and they were convinced that, if my fractured leg had healed, the bone was surely shattered again. They also told me that the manipulation had stirred me sufficiently from my reverie to unleash a stream of expletives at Mr Parker.

During my army career I had, of course, often let fly verbally at officers and NCOs, but always underneath my breath. I was even careful not to let my lips twitch and to maintain a neutral expression, lest I be put on a charge for 'dumb insolence'. I was therefore dismayed that, when I had openly given vent to my feelings, I should have directed the spleen at somebody I respected. At his next week's round of inspection, my grovelling apology was accepted by Mr Parker with a slight smile indicating that this sort of thing was not uncommon.

After I had recovered my senses, I found that it was only my lower leg that was encased in a light plaster, so my manoeuvrability had been considerably increased. For the first time since July, I was able to survey the world from an upright position, albeit the somewhat wobbly stance of standing on one leg by the side of my bed. As with the explorers of old, new worlds were soon opening up to me and, with the aid of a wheelchair, I made a ground-breaking visit to the bathroom. Provided that I kept my plastered leg over the side, I could even indulge in the luxury of a bath. Never had my limbs been so grateful to feel the warmth of soapy water, as opposed to the scrubbing down that the weekly blanket bath entailed.

But human nature is never satisfied and I wanted to increase my mobility by hopping on one leg. At first I confined myself to hopping around my bed, but then, like Alexander the Great, I sought new worlds to conquer and my self-imposed challenge was to hop to the loo. Alas, like Field Marshal Montgomery, I had attempted a hop too far and I finished up on the ward floor.

Luckily, no damage was done, but I received a severe dressing down from Sister and, until I graduated to crutches, the wheel-chair was to be my source of locomotion.

Does He Take Sugar?

Some years after the War, a radio programme dealt with some of the problems that face people confined to a wheelchair. It emphasised the point that, too often, the disabled incumbent was referred to in the third person singular, similar to enquiries regarding a pet dog. I am pleased to say that I was never the victim of such discourtesy. Indeed, people spoke to me directly and seemed genuinely concerned about my progress.

On that historic day, when I made my first wheelchair sortie into Worksop, I remember feeling as excited as I did when, as a young boy, I was allowed to make my first solo venture to the nearby shops. It was great to see some of the town's features, which had been central to many of the anecdotes of the up patients. In addition to the attraction of the cinema, a favourite spot was the restaurant at the local Co-op, where one could obtain a good fish and chips tea for half a crown (12.5p). Such a meal was a welcome break from the monotonous hospital fare, but small as the sum seems today, the price in real terms was not cheap.

Luckily, the Co-op possessed a lift to the restaurant and my friends were able to push me into the dining area without too much trouble. But there was always a certain amount of ado, as doors were propped open and various obstacles removed from my path. On one occasion, when my group had made it to a table, a lady sitting nearby called one of my group over to her. At first, I thought she was going to complain at our somewhat noisy entrance. But no, she explained that her son was serving some-where with the army in Europe and, if we were not offended, she would like to pay for our meal.

This was the second time I had experienced this type of kind-ness and my mind turned back to almost exactly a year before when, in a pub in North London, my friend Roly was 'adopted', with the resulting drinks all round. I have often thought of these incidents and how the donors must have yearned for their own kin to be present, rather than the need to adopt substitutes.

What is it like in London?

I was able to put this question to my parents when they came to see me at the beginning of November. They tended to make light of the situation for, in addition to the deadly V2 rockets, there had been a number of air raids – albeit nothing like the scale of the 1940 Blitz. As usual, my father was optimistic, convinced as ever that Hitler was running out of resources, which was now becoming increasingly true.

There were two encouraging signs that the War was coming to an end. One was the announcement that the stringent blackout regulations, which had been enforced even before the start of hostilities, were to be relaxed to those of a 'dim-out'. Naked lights could still not be shown but, provided that curtains were drawn, all would be well with the air raid wardens. The song 'I'm Going to Get Lit Up when the Lights Go on in London' suddenly became popular again.

The other encouraging piece of news was that, from the end of the year, the Home Guard was to be stood down. Clearly, the danger of invasion was now over and the debate began concerning how effective Dad's Army would have been had the Germans arrived.

About a fortnight after my parents' last visit, I received an unexpected afternoon visit from my mother. She had left home at some unearthly hour in order to make a one-day trip to see me, as she was concerned about the welfare of my brother, who was serving in Italy. He had sent my mother an unusual type of letter, saying that he would not be writing for a while. At the same time, he had also enclosed a letter to be forwarded to me, as he did not know my latest address. So, my mum wanted to know what was going on.

The simple answer was that my brother had developed an abscess on his right arm requiring his hospitalisation and an operation, which could make writing difficult. He did not wish to worry our mother by telling her that we were both in dock, hence his line of action. But, if he did not wish to worry our mother, his action, although well-intended, had had the reverse effect. Despite his request 'not to tell mum', I had no alternative but to reveal the contents of his letter; my mother's relief was marked.

At this time my mother was fifty-eight years old, but in keeping with people of her generation she was much older physically than latter-day generations. She stayed to have a cup of tea and, after further chit-chat, told me that she was worried about dad and she should be getting back. As she walked through the ward doors on her way home, I felt both ashamed and angry. Here was my mother about to take a wartime railway journey to a bomb-strafed London and I was unable even to escort her to the station. My anger was directed at the War itself. How many people all over Europe were suffering worries and, in many cases, enduring serious deprivations? But I was brought back to earth by a nurse asking me if I wanted to have my back rubbed.

Although I was now able to get up, a lot of my time was spent in bed and, in order to avoid bedsores, it was the practice of the time for bed patients to have the base of their spine rubbed with diluted surgical spirit. The nurse did her round as part of the ward routine. But routines are often interrupted and, on one occasion, one of the lads made an improper suggestion. The fool should have realised just how vulnerable he was, for our nurse responded to his advances by becoming somewhat careless with her application of the surgical spirit. The result was that certain tender parts of his male anatomy were splashed, creating the same sensation as applying iodine to an open cut.

After his cries eventually subsided, he remained very quiet for the best part of a week. But colleagues constantly teased him by asking whether or not he was going to have his back rubbed that day.

Jingle Bombs, Jingle Bombs, Jingle all the way!

The month of December was like the curate's egg: good in parts, but, in this case, good in the first half, bad in the second. I had now graduated to using crutches, which I found to be a strange experience. But, after a few strength taxing trips to the main gate of the hospital, I became reasonably mobile, which was a much better condition in which to enjoy life.

As Christmas approached, the festive spirit began to prevail and a number of particularly enjoyable visits from a local concert party took place. It was a delight to watch young girls and lads dancing and singing, even if words were sometimes forgotten. One of the members of the group had a particularly good voice, and I always think of the group whenever I hear the song, 'I'm Taking a Trip California Way'.

In addition to such visits, we received invitations from local firms to their Christmas parties and my newly-found mobility enabled me to go. The firms even arranged transport and all of us were treated in a most generous fashion at a time when most consumer items were in short supply.

To add to this time of good cheer, I seemed to be making good progress at chatting up one of the nurses to whom I had lost my heart. All the signs looked good regarding the fast-approaching time when I would become even more mobile, for I realised that I was still incapable of sweeping the floor, let alone sweeping an attractive young lady off her feet.

Then everything started to go wrong. My budding romance nosedived into a no-hope situation when chatting up was superseded by shutting up. Also, the atmosphere in the ward changed as most of the up patients left on Christmas leave, which resulted in a nasty half-empty feeling prevailing.

Then, out of the blue, on the 16th the Germans launched an offensive in the Ardennes. In the first instance it was mainly the Americans forces who were temporarily sent reeling from the surprise attack, which developed into the Battle of the Bulge. This event was a madcap idea of Hitler's, who thought he could repeat his successes of 1940; namely, drive a wedge between the Allied armies, break through to the coast and retake Antwerp. Although there was a general feeling that this would prove impossible, there was concern that something could go horribly wrong. We did not know it, but Christmas Eve witnessed the furthest point of the German advance.

Christmas Day was on a Monday that year, but all over the holiday weekend a heavy atmosphere predominated. An ominous curtain raiser was that during the Saturday/Sunday night, a V1 flying bomb, 'piggy-backed' from a heavier aeroplane, made its noisy way overhead en route to Nottingham. Was Worksop to be the next target? All of this was most disappointing. One moment it seemed that Germany was on the ropes, the next she was fighting back.

I am always nostalgic at Christmas and this occasion was no exception. As I lay in bed that night, my memory turned to the times when rip-roaring parties had been the order of the day, while here I was in bed before 9 p.m. But, before I dissolved into an orgy of self-pity, my mind turned to the disappointment of those British troops who had been recalled from Christmas leave in order to help plug the gap in the Ardennes that the Germans were desperately seeking to expand. But, somehow, things seemed so much brighter on Boxing Day.

Until about 1973, the Christmas holiday period was of short duration, it being confined to Christmas Day itself and Boxing Day. New Years' Day was not a holiday, except in Scotland, so in 1944 it was back to the normal routine on the Wednesday. Patients began to return from leave and one such patient was in trouble, for he had found that his full-length plaster had limited his prowess on the dance floor. Ever resourceful, he had cut off the piece above the knee, which meant that he could now perform some nifty steps. But, during his Saturday morning round, Mr Parker was definitely not amused at this development, and he demanded to know from the patient how the plaster cast had come to be damaged. The reply was quite clever, insofar as it was difficult to disprove. Our budding dancer claimed that he had had to dive to the floor when a buzz bomb had landed nearby and the plaster had thereby become a casualty. Mr Parker was a liberal-minded man, but he was no fool and he simply did not accept the story. Whether it was a coincidence or not, the patient was quickly exiled to a less friendly hospital.

It was now only days away from the new year and I realised that the changes that had ensued during the past twelve months were outstanding. To think it was such a short time ago that I was enjoying the delights of the Otley ballroom and preparing myself for a frosty tour of the Yorkshire moors. All this seemed to belong to ancient history. But periods of being seemingly stuck for good in some forsaken spot, then experiencing rapid changes, were features of army life.

But enough of the past. What would 1945 have in store?

Watching the War Wind Down

As the wireless heralded the arrival of 1945, we all went a little mad, kissed the nurses and had a few tipples from the various bottles that had been obtained for the occasion. Tony, our Italian former prisoner of war now promoted co-belligerent, was clear in his belief. '1945, c'est la fin de la guerre,' he cried joyfully in his fluent French. But many of us were not so convinced that the War would end in the new year, and we were not alone, for neither did some very well-informed people. Accounts of the Big Three Power conference held in Yalta a month later reveal that the early defeat of Germany was not to be expected.[1]

It was clear that the Germans had wasted precious men and materials in their abortive Christmas Ardennes offensive. Field Marshal Montgomery, who had been given temporary command over all northern Allied ground forces, was not slow to explain publicly how he had restored the situation, and in so doing he upset the leading American generals with his patronising manner. Meanwhile, in north-west Europe the fighting was severe. Although the Ardennes offensive had weakened the Germans, there remained the obstacles of the Siegfried Line and the Rhine for the Allies to overcome before Germany could be entered in force. On the eastern front, the Red Army had still to cross the Vistula and had some way to go before Berlin was a realistic target.

The Far Eastern situation looked even less promising. A long series of costly island-hopping invasions seemed inevitable before mainland Japan could be tackled, while in China the War was going badly. China had been fighting a major invasion by Japan since 1937, but the civil war between Chiang Kai Shek, leader of the Nationalist forces, and the Chinese Red Army continued. This conflict, which was not finally settled until 1949, flared up in late 1944, weakened Chinese resistance and enabled the Japanese

---

[1] Taylor, *English History 1914–1945*.

to take advantage of the situation. So, while the ending of the war in Europe in 1945 seemed just about possible, the difficulties in the Sino-Japanese situation made the Allied war against Japan look certain to continue well into 1946.

To add to the problems in the main theatres of war, at the end of 1944 a difficult situation had developed in Greece, which continued into the new year. Almost simultaneously with the Germans being forced out of Greece, serious fighting that involved British troops had taken place, as the left-wing guerrilla groups had risen in revolt against the possible restoration of the Greek king and, to them, the imposition of an unacceptable government.

Churchill had flown to Athens on Christmas day (1944), determined not to let Greece fall under Communist rule. After a considerable amount of arm-twisting, he succeeded in persuading the conflicting Greek parties to reach a compromise. But would the fragile agreement that he managed to broker fail and result in delays in the main task of fighting the Germans?

Back in Worksop there was no sympathy for the Greek rebels. The general feeling was that any action which involved unnecessary loss of British lives should be condemned. I remember a fellow patient claiming that all the Greek rebels should be shot. Somebody always had a simple solution to any problem, however detailed.

Can Spring be far Behind?

Those of us who felt gloomy about the situation and the prospects for an early peace felt even more depressed as the January weather worsened and trips into town, when one had to rely upon a wheel-chair or crutches for at least part of the journey, were virtually impossible. But, despite all the misgivings, the situation was to change with a speed that revealed how dangerous it is to make political and military predictions.

In the middle of the month, and despite the weather, the Red Army launched a massive offensive that carried it across the Vistula and brought Berlin into foreseeable striking distance. This offensive clearly revealed the failing powers of the German army and was a major factor in deciding the 'who is going to be first to get to Berlin' question.

As the Red Army was making rapid progress across Poland and into Germany, a controversial raid by the RAF upon the historic town of Dresden took place. The policy of Air Marshal 'Bomber' Harris was to try to bomb the Germans into submission, and this strategy has remained a subject of post-war debate concerning its effectiveness and the moral issues involved. Many German cities had been devastated, but the Dresden raid raised the question of whether it was necessary to attack a historical town that had no strategic importance? Or was the raid undertaken for political reasons to make the point to the advancing Red Army that Britain was heavily involved in German affairs and wanted to make its presence felt?

While the War was still being waged with frightening intensity, the atmosphere in the ward was lightened by the arrival of two newcomers, Mickey and 'Dizzy'. Mickey was the nephew of a famous comedian and was a funny man in his own right. Dizzy had some unpronounceable Italian surname from which his nickname was derived. His father was a Church of England vicar, but Dizzy's wild activities indicated there was little likelihood of his following father's holy footsteps.

Both Mickey and Dizzy were perfect foils for each other and had us all in fits of laughter until the night sister brought down the curtain on their act by insisting on silence. After enjoying their antics we felt that the War was miles away. But like most comedians each of our star performers had his serious side.

One morning, Dizzy approached my bed with a grim look on his face and a letter in his hand. At first I thought that one of his ex-girlfriends had caught up with him, but the matter was far more serious. Before he was wounded, Dizzy had served in the Service Corps dropping supplies by air to advanced Allied troops. On his last trip, while he and his team were busy pushing material out of their aircraft, an enemy plane swooped and commenced to shoot them up. Dizzy was not too badly hurt albeit the attack left him with a pronounced stutter. But the man next to him was killed immediately. The father of this poor man had written to Dizzy, via the Red Cross, as there were various uncertainties in the reports concerning his son's fate; he nursed a hope that his son was still alive.

'How,' stammered Dizzy, 'am I to answer this one?' And he asked me to help him draft a reply. So for most of the morning we faced the unpleasant task of compiling a letter confirming the son's death, but stressing the inadequate consolation that his ending was instantaneous. In this exercise there was nothing of the clown about Dizzy.

Mickey was a barber in Civvy Street and in the late 1960s I chanced to enter the West End salon where he worked. After greetings of recognition, Mickey began to reflect upon the War as he snipped away at my greying locks. He still had his sense of humour, but behind the banter it was clear that the War had left him deeply scarred.

The Bones have Knitted

February 1945 saw some good progress concerning my own condition. The light plaster and bandages on my damaged leg were removed and, for the first time, I was able to see what had been done to me. I realised that any hopes that I may have entertained of winning a shapely legs contest at some holiday camp competition had sunk without trace. At the same time as the plaster was removed, I was supplied with soft boots and a calliper, complete with an attachment to the heel of the right boot to stop my foot from dragging. I was now told to stand on both feet and I took my first faltering steps around my bed.

It was quite a strange sensation having to learn to walk again, which involved overcoming problems of balance and the gradual lengthening of one's range before collapsing from fatigue. In the first few days the use of crutches seemed so much easier and far less painful, but I began to feel like Jack the lad as, with the aid of a stick, my mobility increased. As the weather improved, I began to visit the town on most afternoons. Transport for most of the journey was by bus, and I cannot remember ever paying a fare. The 'clippies' seemed to regard charging service personnel from the hospital as being against their trade union's rules.

The cinema, which was cheap in real terms, the Co-op restaurant, the pub and the company of certain off-duty nurses helped to compensate for months of bed and restricted activities. On the war fronts, everything seemed to be going well, with the

Germans being taken prisoner in large numbers. Peace could not be far away. But underlying this positive atmosphere, I was also concerned with my future. Was I to remain in the army and be returned to my unit, which seemed unlikely; be transferred to some non-combat section such as the Pay Corps; or be discharged altogether from HM Forces? Before any decision was reached, I had quite a traumatic weekend.

That Wobbly Weekend

My increased mobility had made it possible for me to apply for leave to go home for a weekend. So, on Saturday, 17 March, I stood rather anxiously on the platform at Worksop station. My anxiety stemmed from the knowledge that V2 rockets were still dropping on London. The war in Europe was obviously ending and my luck so far had been reasonably good, but was it to run out at the twelfth hour? As the train I had boarded neared London, my worries increased.

During the War, I had never nursed ambitions to win the Victoria Cross or even the Military Medal, but I was able to keep under reasonable control the fears that most people experienced. In the 1940 onslaught on London, I had sufficient courage – or stupidity – to become 'Blitz-wise', knowing when danger was imminent and when to take shelter. Until my luck ran out in Normandy, I had been quickly learning to duck and dive and not to jump at the least unexpected sound. But I had now lost this balance and, to put it crudely, I was in a blue funk.

This funk was not altogether unfounded. Well after the War, I learnt from a TV programme that the last of the V2s to fall on London killed, among others, a soldier home on leave from the Far East. This was the type of fate that I dreaded on that March weekend leave. I understand that, as the War's end grew nearer, well-trained veterans at the front grew increasingly apprehensive, so I was not alone in my fears.

In the railway carriage on my journey home was a group of young members of the Women's Royal Naval Service (WRNS) and I quickly appreciated my changed status. Whereas I had usually vacated my seat on a public vehicle in favour of an elderly or disabled person, seated passengers were now making room for me. A charming member of the group moved over to sit on a suitcase in order that I could sit down. None of the group seemed at all concerned about the V2s and the conversation ranged from trivia to serious wartime matters. Before long, the train arrived at King's Cross station.

Much of my youth had been spent in the King's Cross area, for it was the location of my youth club and a place where numerous friends lived. As I waited for the trolley bus to take me home, everything looked different, albeit there was no noticeable new bomb damage. The very buildings seemed tired and war weary, but perhaps that was how I was feeling.

Electrically-driven trolley buses, which were a common form of transport in London before the War, were notorious for their rapid acceleration. The conductor, quick to realise that I was unsteady on my feet, gave me a hand to my seat; another example of my changed status. Before long, the bus arrived in my home district of Kentish Town. Ten months is a long time in warfare and I limped home a somewhat wiser person from the young man who felt that the Second Front should be opened immediately, if not sooner.

A number of relatives dropped in to see me and the conversation made me realise what home-based Londoners had gone through during my absence. Among the relatives, I was pleased to meet my friend and cousin Nobby, who was home on leave from the army and who was to give me much-needed support in the next few days.

That evening Nobby and I visited the youth club that had played an important part in both our lives, but few people who we knew were there. Then we moved on to one of our favourite pubs, 'The Camden Stores', which was always referred to as 'The Jerry'. Why it was so-called nobody knew, but it was unique in many ways.

The Jerry was small, almost tiny, being a converted Victorian residential house. Into its small bar, it seemed that half the drinking population of the proletarian section of the Regent's Park area would cram, especially on a Saturday night. Standing shoulder to shoulder with other customers presented some difficulties, insofar as lifting one's glass to imbibe required considerable manoeuvring. Around the edges of the bar were a few chairs that, by an unspoken law, were reserved for the ladies, many of whom were the mothers of old friends of ours. A piano in the corner would give out a range of songs old and new that added to a very noisy but friendly atmosphere. It was this atmosphere, and the fact that most of the customers had known each other for years, that made the pub so popular.

Nobby and I arrived just as the evening was getting under way, and I had nursed misgivings that I would prove incapable of coping with the usual push and shove scenario. But I need not have worried for, by some miraculous means, a path was cleared for me and the seated mums moved up to make room. All these actions were very kind, but they hurt me as they rubbed in the reality of my disability.

Sunday morning was right for a lie-in and as Nobby, who had slept in my absent brother's bed, and I were lazily contemplating getting up, a V2 fell. It landed some distance away, and there was no warning of any kind. This I found particularly disturbing, but neither Nobby nor my parents seemed concerned.

Throughout the Sunday and Monday, Nobby acted as my minder as we did the rounds of the cinema and old-time haunts. But, on the Monday evening, Nobby's leave was up. Alone, I paid a visit to the parents of my friend Roly, whose father I found a most interesting person. After a pleasant evening, he insisted on seeing me to the bus stop.

I have often reflected upon this weekend about which, some sixty years later, I have such clear memories. Were my fears manifestly obvious? I shall never know, but the weekend reinforced my knowledge of the fickle qualities of courage.

At long last, Tuesday arrived and, about midday, I was again at King's Cross station. During my time in the army, I had always avoided station farewells for they are so emotionally disturbing. But this time my mother insisted on seeing me off.

As the train pulled out, I felt deeply ashamed of myself. Here was my poor old mum remaining in a danger zone, while I was wishing the train to accelerate and get me into comparative safety. The fact that I could have taken no other action, for I was still subject to military law and had no alternative other than to return from leave, gave me no consolation. I felt a coward, glad to be running away from danger.

Farewell to Worksop

Events moved at a rapid pace shortly after my return to Worksop. Four days later, Saturday, 24 March, the Western Allied forces crossed the Rhine without too much difficulty and with comparatively light casualties. Any hopes of their getting to Berlin before the Russians had faded, for the Red Army had made some spectacular advances and was beginning the main assault on the German capital. But, even with these hammer blows from the east and west, it was thought that the centre of German resistance would move from Berlin to some remote forest area highly suitable for defence and cause the War to drag out for a few more months.

While the War was being settled, my fate lay in the hands of the Invaliding Medical Board, before which I had to attend on 27 March and naturally I was apprehensive about the outcome. After my leg was examined, a great deal of medical mumbo jumbo ensued. A corporal was taking notes all the time and, when the doctors were finished with me, he said, 'That's it, this means your ticket.' My army days were over.

As papers and forms of all shapes and sizes concerning my demobilisation were being completed, I was experiencing mixed feelings. Officially, I was still in the army until the expiration of my demob leave, which had been determined as 30 May, just two days after my 21st birthday. But, to all intents and purposes, I was now a civilian.

My first reaction was one of relief and I felt like a man released from prison. Within the constraints of the law, the mores of society, and the need to earn a living, I would henceforth be free to operate. No longer would I have to stand to attention at the behest of some NCO or officer, nor be subjected to humiliating punishment for a minor infringement of stupid barrack rules. If I felt unwell, I would be able to lie in bed without the rigmarole of reporting sick. I could stay out all night without fear of having to report back to a hostile guardroom. Such were some of my immediate thoughts as my discharge was being processed.

But was the army not good in at least some parts? Had I not learnt something useful for future life and helpful for my development as a person? And what of my army friends? Were they to be left behind, cast aside like a pair of old boots?

On balance, I remained happy and excited and it was in this mood that I returned to the hospital and began informing family and friends of my news. I also had to tell the nurse, with whom I had been enjoying the highlights of the town, of my fate. She had already been invited to a colleague's wedding, taking place in London in early May, so we knew we would be meeting in the near future. But, meanwhile, we were determined to make the most of my remaining Worksop days.

There were still various matters to be completed before my discharge, one of which was to be measured for my demob suit. On exit from the forces, men were supplied with a suit, a pair of shoes, a hat and a fairly liberal supply of clothing coupons to kit oneself out for civilian life. In addition, everybody received a gratuity, which was determined by one's rank and length of service.

So that I could receive a suit that paid some respect to the contours of my body, I had to travel to a centre in nearby Nottingham to be measured. If I remember rightly, one was given little choice over colour or pattern; only one's measurements seemed to matter. I was told that all my gear would be sent to my home in London, so I made my way back to the hospital, wondering what kind of sartorial splendour awaited me.

The next few days were spent in a whirl of saying goodbye to the staff and civilians that I had got to know during my eight months stay. I was particularly sad to say farewell to Steve, a friend of the ward who had performed many acts of kindness for us patients. The day before my departure was 12 April, a day that was to go down in history, not because of my leaving Worksop – I modestly add – but for an event on the other side of the Atlantic.

'Terrible news, ain't it?' the taxi driver said as he took me on my last return trip to the hospital. For one dreadful moment my heart sank. Had some catastrophe occurred to reverse the trend of the rapidly approaching end to the war in Europe? 'Roosevelt was such a good man,' my taxi driver continued, 'and now he's dead.'

I felt a huge feeling of relief for, although I respected Franklin DR as a liberal anti-Nazi United States President, his death was unlikely to delay the victory that was so near. Nobody knew anything about the new President, Harry Truman.

Any Friday the 13th is deemed to be unlucky, but the one that occurred in April of that year was an exception to the rule as far as I was concerned. My final farewells were said and I was off home to try to pick up the pieces that had been thrown into the air some two-and-a-half years previously when I had become 14405896. My stay in Worksop was one that I shall never forget. The people were kind and I had matured considerably. My education was still at a low level, but at least I had become aware of what I had to attempt.

On my journey home, I remembered Remarque's book, *The Road Back* and his story of a group of young German soldiers returning to civilian life after the 1914–18 conflict. When their attempts to regain their pre-war happiness and ways of life had failed, they concluded that they had to find not the road back, but the road forward. It was a point to bear in mind as, once more, the train pulled in to King's Cross.

Summertime, but Victory is Elusive

'It's all quiet now, mate,' said the porter at King's Cross station, in answer to my query as to how things were progressing. 'Nothing's dropped for the last couple of weeks,' he added. It was reassuring news and so good to hear expressed in true London style. The whole atmosphere seemed so different from that grey day less than a month previously, when I had arrived for that nail-biting weekend.

Before long, I was at home and receiving a warm welcome from my parents. Although they had seen me in the recent past, we realised that a new chapter of life was about to open. My brother was still in the Middle East, but leave rosters were getting into their stride, so it should not be too long before his turn came up.

A box of goodies awaited me: my demob suit. With much trepidation I tried it on, fearing that I would look nothing like the man in the 'Walk the Willoughby Way' advertisements that were common just before the War. But I was in for a pleasant surprise for, as my dear old grandmother said, I looked a toff.

Much of my former civilian gear still fitted me and fashion in that period, especially for men, had taken a back seat. So I did not look too strange when I turned out that evening in my earlier clothing. Perhaps only the calliper on my leg and my use of a walking stick indicated my changed status.

Victory in Europe (VE Day) was still some four weeks away and the anticipation was electric. But when would it come? The pubs were full, despite beer and all alcoholic drinks being in short supply. A main worry was whether or not there would be enough drink for the parties being planned for when Johnny came marching home and for VE Day itself.

Each day Allied prisoner-of-war camps were being liberated and the newspapers carried photographs of houses festooned with welcome home signs and bunting, which must have been saved from some pre-war event. Shots appeared of men returning from years of captivity and embracing their wives and children, some of whom had no memories of their fathers.

But not all homecomings were happy events. Many marriages had cracked under the strain of separation, and the returning husband found that he had 'been jacked in for a civvy.' On the other hand, waiting wives sometimes found themselves let down when their men folk had formed liaisons with other women. The expression 'wartime marriage' became synonymous with a hasty and temporary affair.

My old friend Roly was home on leave and we spent numerous evenings together. But he soon had to return and I resorted to the cinema for entertainment. I well remember going to see a light piece of nonsense starring Bing Crosby and Betty Hutton. From the cavorting around in the musical scenario, the programme progressed to the customary newsreel – the change was dramatic.

Instead of feasting our eyes upon beautiful girls and lavish Hollywood escapism, the audience was suddenly plunged into the depths of the depravities of man, as the liberation of the Belsen concentration camp unfolded. Skeletal figures appeared wearing bizarre apparel and picking at their clothing in feeble efforts to delouse themselves. But worse was to come. The camera switched to piles of naked human corpses lying in the most grotesque positions. Occasionally the commentator would draw attention to the twitching of a body, which indicated that death had still to come and some unfortunates had just been dumped and left to expire.

Further newsreel shots were equally horrible. One saw British soldiers, with handkerchiefs tied over their faces, using bulldozers to push heaps of bodies into hastily-dug mass graves. Disinfectant was being liberally scattered to reduce the risk of disease. Only the pungent smell that prevailed was absent from the replication of this dreadful scene. By this time there was not a dry eye in the cinema.

The newsreel continued by showing former guards, women as well as men, being paraded. Among them was the camp commandant, the Beast of Belsen, Joseph Kramer, He was later executed for crimes against humanity, as was the 'Beastess,' Irma Grese.

In conclusion, German civilians were shown who had been compelled to witness the deeds that their government had perpetrated. How proud they must have felt![1]

I wiped my eyes and tottered out of the cinema. Suddenly all the Allied suffering that the War had entailed seemed justified. What would the position have been had Nazi Germany triumphed and gained supremacy in Europe? What horrors would have ensued had a Vichy-type government been jackbooted into Number 10? How many anti-Nazis would have been thrown into some Belsen-style Dartmoor extermination camp? How long would it have been before European Emperor Hitler would have sought to conquer the rest of the world?

When I returned home, I was in a very sober mood. But waiting for me was a former youth club member. Chick, as he was nicknamed, had joined the merchant navy in 1940 and, despite his comparative long service at sea, had never been torpedoed, nor engaged in any naval action. There was always a great deal of luck concerning where one was and at what time.

This somewhat trite observation is borne out by remembering that, as Chick and I were reminiscing in comparative safety, Allied soldiers were still dying on the western front, while in Berlin a most savage battle was raging to take the city. Some thirty thousand Russians lost their lives before the Red Flag was hoisted over the Reichstag and many more sustained terrible wounds.[2]

On the German side, nearly every male, old and young, was thrown hopelessly against the Red Army, with disastrous results for them. But this did not concern us unduly, and we were not worried about the reports of Russian looting and mass rape. A general British reaction was that the Germans were now getting a taste of the appalling treatment they had inflicted upon innocent people in the countries they had ruthlessly invaded.

April ended with Hitler committing suicide. But reports of the event were shrouded in doubt by theories that he was still alive, had gone into hiding, and was ready to emerge when the time was ripe.[3]

---

[1] For a comprehensive account of Nazi atrocities see Cesarani, *The Final Solution; origin and implementation*, London and New York, 1994.

[2] Beevor, *Berlin, the Downfall, 1945*.

[3] Trevor Roper explains the reasons for the doubts which arose in *The Last Days of Hitler*.

Throughout his political life, Hitler had denounced the 'November Criminals', namely the German leaders who had surrendered in 1918. When challenged, as to what he would have done, he replied that he would have gone down fighting. Now he lived true to his intentions and, in so doing, brought about the total foreign occupation and the complete humiliation of his adopted country.

Just how many millions of deaths Hitler had upon his hands is impossible to say, not to mention all the pain and suffering that his actions had caused. Funnily enough, I cannot remember the 1941 song, 'When That Man is Dead and Gone' being revived. Possibly our eyes were fixed on that elusive victory declaration.

May Day and Dancing round the Lamp-posts

In the early days of May, I was best man at the wedding of a former fellow hospital patient, Vic, to his nurse Frankie. My favourite nurse was also present, so a good time was promised. The ceremony and immediate celebrations were held in Richmond, a delightful town on the Thames where Vic's parents lived. The happy couple were going to take a delayed honeymoon, so a little gang of us had time to extend the festivities.

A great and historic weekend lay ahead. On the Saturday evening (5 May) we took ourselves to the Hammersmith Palais de Danse, better known as the 'Hammy Pally'. It was a popular venue, with a band playing smoochy music for lovers to dance close together, but the numbers were interspersed with lively tunes for the energetic. It was a pleasure to watch the execution of some wild and amazing dance routines, but the most that I could manage was a slow waltz.

Suddenly, the music was halted and the master of ceremonies announced that Berlin had fallen. Unlike the scenes in the Boer War, when theatre performances were interrupted with the news that Mafeking had been relieved and the audiences went wild with delight, the news about Berlin only raised a perfunctory cheer. No doubt this was because, with the daily surrender of sections of the German army and the progress of the Russians, the fall of the capital was only to be expected.

Over that weekend, all kinds of reports and rumours of the

back stabbings of the surviving Nazi hierarchy circulated; just who was in charge of the German government? But on the Monday (7th) this question became academic, when it was announced that the German armies had surrendered in both the east and west. Victory was to be celebrated during the following two days.

If the news of the fall of Berlin had been received with comparative calm, that of the victory was ecstatic. On the Monday evening people flocked into the open. There was not only dancing in the streets but lovemaking in many nooks and crannies that overjoyed couples discovered. The pubs were crowded, reserved English gentlemen shook hands with strangers without the formality of introductions, and some individuals just cried with emotion.

Events carried on with increased fervour the following day, when huge crowds gathered in Whitehall and around Buckingham Palace. The fountains in Trafalgar Square were invaded by revellers who cared naught for getting wet. I kept well away from such centres, but decided that I should leave Richmond for a few hours to pay a flying visit to my parents in Kentish Town. Public transport was running a Sunday service.

Neighbours who I had not seen for years came out to celebrate. In the bar at the bottom of my street, somebody started singing and we went through the repertoire of nostalgic war songs. Between numbers, my parents and I raised our glasses to what we had gone through. I had survived one World War, but they had survived two. In addition, their inter-war period, dominated by a worldwide economic depression, had hardly been sweetness and light. But Richmond was calling and I took a rather emotional departure from my folks; albeit a very different one from my departure on my twentieth birthday almost exactly one year earlier, when the Second Front was imminent.

If adults had gone to town on the Tuesday, it was the kiddies' turn on the Wednesday. It seemed that from out of nowhere trestle tables full of sandwiches, cakes, and soft drinks materialised. Obviously, some parents had been planning well in advance and obtained all kind of permits from the local food office. Many adults joined in the spirit of the occasion and organised games, clowned around, and helped things go with a swing.

But gradually the tempo slackened and, if the kiddies were not tired by this time, many of the adults certainly were. Then there was the horrible realisation that there would be some kind of return to work the next day.

So, on 10 May, exactly five years after Hitler's forces had crashed through the Ardennes, large numbers of Londoners, somewhat bleary-eyed, could be seen making half-hearted attempts to break through on the work front.

My girlfriend had to return to Worksop, and we said goodbye knowing that it was unlikely we should meet again. Political differences had arisen and we sensed that they, and the distance between London and Worksop, would prove too much. The final curtain came down in an exchange of letters a week or so later.

Reality Looms Large

As I returned home from Richmond, I realised that it was nearly a month since I had left hospital. But it had all been a whirl of unfolding events: the homecoming, Vic's wedding, and VE Day itself. On the bus, I did some backward and forward thinking. The positive victory celebrations were clearly in mind, but my thoughts were of a negative nature. How, I wondered, did my next-bed neighbour in the Harlow Wood hospital who had lost both of his legs celebrate VE Day? What of the loved ones of my former comrades who had been killed? How had they celebrated their permanent absence?

And what of the next of kin of those who had been posted missing? Possibly, they were suffering the greatest degree of mental anguish as, encouraged by the return of stragglers from the camps, they feverishly hoped that their loved ones would materialise. How cruel for relatives to be let down when a similar name was referred to, or the appearance of a 'lookalike' caused hopes to soar.

Then, of course, there was the continuing war against Japan to be considered. While we had been celebrating, how many Allied prisoners of war were suffering the atrocious conditions that later caused the Western world to gasp in horror? Obviously, the victory in Europe deserved celebrating, but a few moments of reflection showed that the rejoicing necessitated heavy qualification.

I reached home, sank into bed and slept for a good ten hours. When I came up for air and gathered my thoughts, the calendar told me that I had just twenty days of my demob leave left. After the 30th of the month, I would no longer be subject to military law, but neither would I be on the army's payroll. So I had better recover from the hectic times of my leave so far and prepare myself for a return to work.

For several weeks, I had been able to walk without the assistance of my calliper. The muscles near my ankle had strengthened with my greater mobility, and I could walk without my foot dragging. A visit to the orthopaedic hospital confirmed that my calliper was no longer necessary, and I then contacted the Post Office doctor. He thought that I could return to work, but on light duties. This meant that I was not to undertake deliveries and collections, nor any work that involved much walking.

About this time I received a letter from the Ministry of Pensions informing me that I had been awarded an interim disability pension of thirty per cent. This amounted to 12s. 6d. (62.5p in new money) per week. This apparently derisory sum was not so small when one realises that, at that time, a male weekly wage of £5–6 was regarded as reasonably good. Thus opened my dealings with the Ministry, which leads me into making a few observations.

I had heard all kinds of horror stories from First World War veterans concerning the tactics used by the Ministry. It seemed that Scrooge was its patron saint. Accounts abounded of the deserving disabled being tricked into selling their benefits for a mess of potage. I experienced no such skulduggery. On the contrary, numerous documents explained my rights and detailed the welfare services that were available.

Unless there is a loss of a limb or faculty, it is difficult to assess precisely the degree of a disability. Obviously some claimants experience suffering greater than their scars suggest. On the other hand, there are claimants immobile from Monday to Friday, but able to play football over the weekend. Are Ministry doctors to believe all that claimants tell them, or regard them all as lying twisters?

Then there are the problems of the delayed results of front

line activity. Men who were physically wounded were taken out of the line, those who were not carried on for nerves to fray and health to be undermined. A week may be a long time in politics; at the front it can be an eternity. And what of the ex-prisoners of war who, for years after their release, had the recurring nightmare that they were back in their camps?

Perhaps there should be a pension for all who experienced active service? But it would require great wisdom to work out an equitable system.

I have two further criticisms of the present system. First, and here I must declare a vested interest, I consider it unfair that the amount of an award should depend upon the rank of the pensioner when he or she was in the forces. Why should a disabled private draw less than an officer given that the degree of disability is the same? Secondly, it is clear to me that those who are represented at tribunals by competent individuals, or bodies such as the British Legion, have a better chance of securing a just settlement than more inarticulate claimants.

While I was becoming actively concerned with such issues, British politicians were facing the fact that the party unity that had prevailed throughout the greater part of the War was ending. Churchill made efforts to persuade the Labour Party to stay in the coalition government until the war against Japan, then expected to continue for another eighteen months, was over; but, on 28 May – my twenty-first birthday – it was announced that a general election would be held on 5 July. However, in order to include the votes of the returning overseas personnel the results would not be announced until three weeks later.

So, just less than three years after I had delivered my last telegram, I returned to the Post Office wondering whether the Postmaster General would be a Tory or Labour minister.

Back to Work, Back to Basics

The months of June and July 1945 witnessed my return to work, a general election, and my falling in love again. Everybody's expectations were high for, even if Japan had still to be defeated, it was only a matter of time before the complete end of the War. Meanwhile, most of the troops should be coming home and life seemed set to return to something like normal. It was against this optimistic background that I walked on to the sorting office floor of the North-West District branch of the Post Office, where I had previously worked as a boy messenger. I was now a full-blown postman.

Most of my new colleagues were men in their fifties who were too old for military service. When they were younger, many had served in the First World War and a number had been disabled. The regular all-male staff had been supplemented by temporary postwomen.

'Ah, it's young Richie,' cried Jimmy Jenkins and he crossed the floor to shake me warmly by the hand. Two years later I was to be a pall-bearer at Jimmy's funeral.

Ostensibly, Jimmy had died of tuberculosis – which was fairly common in the post-war period – but when his widow came to the office to clear up her late husband's affairs she gave a different explanation. Mrs Jenkins claimed that Jimmy had, in fact, died of a broken heart. Their son had met a horrible death at sea, where he had perished in a blazing oil tanker. She explained that as Jimmy had watched the young men returning from the War, the trickle had soon became a flood; he had been reminded daily that he would never see his lad again. He just could not reconcile himself to his loss.

Several features of Post Office life stand out in my memory. The pre-war deliveries of letters had been cut from six per day to three; the time of the last collection from letterboxes had been changed to from 11 p.m. to 6.30 p.m. All the postwomen were paid less than the men for doing the same job and they enjoyed no pension rights. They knew that, as the men returned, their jobs would go. As for general pay levels, an agreement was reached whereby all wartime supplements would be consolidated into a new wage structure. A postman on the maximum scale would earn £5 15s. per week, (£5.75 in modern money). I well remember that my pay as a young postman was £3 7s. 6d.

Work had its breaks and during the mid-morning interval people tended to gravitate to the same tables to drink their tea, I cannot remember coffee being an alternative. Those with common interests such as gardening, horse racing, sport and nothing in particular would usually sit at the same tables. My choice was the politics group.

The men with whom I sat were old enough to be my father and I was often told that my views would change when I grew older. In my conceit, I thought that such remarks were a poor response to the first-class case I was advocating, which I knew to be absolutely right – Lenin said so.

Many of the disputed issues concerned the Soviet Union and whether or not its demands on Poland, ex-prisoners of war, restrictions on speech and reluctance to join the war against Japan could be justified. On these and other issues, I was a stout defender of the Russians.

One of the group, a chap called Albert, who had lost an arm in the 1914 conflict, was one of my sternest opponents in argument. He was especially critical of the freedom of expression in Russia, and told me that he hoped that we would meet in later years when we would know who was right. This meeting did not transpire but, had it done so, I would have had to admit that Albert was much nearer to reality than me.

Only a privileged few members of the British Communist Party were aware of the true nature of the Stalin regime but, with the end of the war in Europe, more information was circulating that aroused ground-level concern as to the true nature of the situation. But who and what was one to believe? In the pre-war period, had not the Western press over-reached itself with anti-Communist propaganda? Against Western expectations, had not the Russians 'torn the guts out of the German Army'? Had not the Soviet Union broken the chain of capitalism at its weakest link and, in the new post-war period, been about to prove the superiority of socialism?

These points formed the main thrust of the arguments that I was advocating. Perhaps I did not want to know the truth about Stalin, while those British Communist Party leaders who did know were not prepared to tell the rank and file Members.[1]

Despite the different views expressed at the politics table, none of us foresaw the enormous economic, technological and social changes that were to unfurl in the next few decades. A postman's wage of nearly £6 per week was considered fairly good and who could have foreseen that this sum would soon be regarded as derisory? The growth of consumer purchasing power, the advent of television, the extension of the range of durable goods, and such items as holidays abroad were all beyond our wildest expectations. Nor did we appreciate the influence that the War had had upon the peoples of the colonial possessions, who were about to demand, and in most case achieve, their independence.

Meanwhile, we on the politics table began to focus upon the pending election.

The General Election

Churchill was a popular wartime leader and undoubtedly his stand in 1940, when all seemed lost, stood him in good stead for the forthcoming contest. A Tory election poster of a full size photo of Churchill with the slogan, 'Help him to finish the job', was a key feature of the Conservative campaign. Everywhere he went on the election trail he was warmly welcomed, and when Churchill came to nearby Camden Town – a working class area – his success seemed assured.

But there were a number of factors weighing against a Tory victory. The past policies of the Conservative Party were seen as contributing to the economic depression of the 1930s, in which some terrible hardships were endured, especially in the industrial areas. The Means Test and the cutting of relief benefits to subsistence levels were harsh measures that fell mainly on

---

[1] Beckett, *Enemy Within: The Rise and Fall of the British Communist Party*, 1995.

working class people. In 1945, their memories were still fresh and it was the numerically superior workers who could determine the outcome of the election.[2]

Adding to these criticisms were the charges that the Conservative Party had been led by the 'Men of Munich', whose craven appeasement policies failed to stop the War. When the conflict began, men had been sent off to War badly equipped and badly led. Although most of these charges could not be levelled at Churchill, they could be, and were, directed at his party.

Post Office workers had a special reason for not liking Churchill. The Trades Disputes Act of 1927, passed after the General Strike one year earlier, was seen mainly as the work of Churchill. This vindictive piece of legislation, apart from various anti-trade union measures, forbade the affiliation of all Civil Service unions to the Trades Union Congress and the Labour Party. However, as the War was coming to an end, the Union of Post Office Workers threatened to defy this law and apply for affiliation with the TUC.

Churchill replied that, if the UPW did so, the pension rights of its members would be forfeited. This may have been shadow-boxing by both parties, but it revealed that Churchill had not modified his attitude towards the unions.

I was only eleven years old in 1935, when the last General Election had taken place, and I had taken no part in the various by-elections during the ten-year political truce. The contest of 1945 taught me a great deal about the mechanics of the polls, the power of the press (TV was completely absent) and the multiplicity of factors that help people decide for whom to vote.

And so I was introduced to the delights of political canvassing. For the next three weeks I divided my time working for Dr Jeger, the Labour candidate in South Saint Pancras, helping Gabriel (Bill) Carritt, Communist, in Westminster, and wooing a political young lady whose charms made electioneering far more interesting than otherwise would have been the case.

All canvassers were supplied with a variety of materials, which included promise cards, requests for transport and biographical

---

[2] Calder, *The People's War*, 1969, Chapter 9 gives a useful account of the issues involved in the election.

details of the candidate. As well as an array of rosettes and 'Vote Labour' labels, canvassers were also supplied with tips on what to say and how to say it. Armed with this formidable collection, I sallied forth to convince the workers of Somers Town that the return of the Labour candidate was vital if post-war Britain were to flourish.

With some trepidation and my gambit in the forefront of my mind, I knocked on my first door. A middle-aged man answered, but before I could utter a word he quickly said, 'Not today, thank you,' and just as quickly shut the door. Dismissed like some cheapjack salesman, my hopes to win the constituency for Labour had received a severe blow. But I persisted and just before 9 p.m. the latest time for calling, I reported back to the Committee rooms the number of firm promises, doubtfuls, don't knows, and those who were out. All this information was recorded to be used, I was told, on polling day, 'knocking up' and getting every supporter to the booths.

Within a comparatively short space of time, I learnt some of the pitfalls to avoid, including not spending too much time in argument, or seeking to please those who wanted a cast-iron guarantee that the return of a Labour MP would see the repair of a faulty kitchen-waste pipe. I never encountered any aggression, but I nearly invited retaliation on one occasion when, in answer to my request for political support, a man told me that he was nothing, to which I was tempted to state that this was obvious.

There were situations that one could have done without. When a young child called, 'Mum, there's a strange man at the door!' Or when one was forced to raise one's face and voice against a downpour to shout the virtues of the candidate in answer to the curt demand of, 'who is it?' from an upstairs window on a rainy evening.

On one occasion I raised my arm to knock on the intended door when suddenly the knocker was whisked away as the lady of the house had chosen that precise moment to go out. I wondered why the lady had turned a ghastly shade of pale, until I realised that she had opened her door only to see a strange man before her with his arm raised as if about to deliver a fatal blow. Naturally I apologised profusely and, in an attempt to cover my embarrassment, went quickly into my gambit of how she might vote. But had I struck a vote for Labour? I don't think so!

I gathered that there is no ideal time for canvassing. Call too early in the evening and the potential voter has not arrived home; call later and there is resentment at being disturbed. Sunday morning has its problems. Arrive at say 10.30 and our voter is still in bed, call about noon and he has already left for the pub. And if the man were not available a common reply to a request for a vote from his wife was 'I'll have to ask my husband.' In 1945, Women's Lib had clearly a long way to go.

Meanwhile, back in the committee rooms there would be the frantic activity of envelope stuffing, addressing labels, and deciding which 'doubtfuls' should be seen again. To take a night off to go to the pictures could be seen as betrayal of the revolution.

Westminster Chimes

The electoral policy of the Communist Party was to work for the return of a Labour government, while at the same time running a limited number of its own candidates with the hope that a group of Communist MPs would advocate strong socialist policies in the House. Consequently, in 1945 the party contested twenty seats, one of which was the Westminster Abbey Division, where Bill Carritt was the candidate.

Bill was a wartime soldier, a member of the Fourteenth Army, and had flown home from Burma on special leave to contest the seat. He had stood in the same constituency as an Independent in a by-election in May 1939 when, on an anti-Chamberlain policy, he had the support of such leading Labour personalities as Sir Stafford Cripps, Eleanor Rathbone and J B Priestley.

In a straight fight with the Tory candidate, Carritt received 4,674 votes, 32% of the poll, while the successful Tory received 9,678 votes, 39%.[3] It was remarkable that in a safe Conservative

---

[3] The City of Westminster Archives kindly provided me with the voting figures and drew my attention to a report in the *Westminster and Pimlico News*, 19 May 1939, which read:

seat a left-wing candidate should receive nearly half the number of the votes cast for the successful Tory. What then was the situation in 1945 when Carritt stood as a Communist and, unlike the 1939 by-election, a Labour candidate also contested? I was about to find out.

What surprised me in roaming around the back streets of Westminster were the marked contrasts in this wealthy borough. Behind the glittering West End thoroughfares were examples of grim housing with units that were totally lacking in mod cons.

When I knocked on the doors the responses naturally varied, but those who were totally opposed to the ideas of Communism were few. A common answer to my request for support from anti-Tory voters was that, although there was sympathy for Carritt, most felt that they owed their allegiance to Labour and it was this fear of splitting the anti-Tory vote that prevented support for the Communist. This was a difficult, if not impossible, nut to crack.

The result was that Carritt received 2,964 votes, 17.6% of the poll, against the Labour candidates 4,408 votes, 26%, and the successful Tory's 9,160 votes, 54%.

To obtain nearly three thousand votes was a creditable performance, but one can see that, in comparison with the 1939 by-election when there was no Labour candidate and Carritt had stood as an Independent, his 1945 vote had been nearly halved. And this was at a time when support for the Communist Party was comparatively high. No doubt the party analysed all the results but, for political reasons it continued to contest elections, only to see deposits being lost with unfailing regularity as the Cold War began to dominate the situation.

Another point I learnt from my first general election was the marked difference between the views of the party leaders and the concerns of individual voters. Often my speech on what a

---

Mr Carritt's big rally packed the Garrick Theatre Charing Cross Road on Monday evening. In a moment of enthusiasm, Mr Richard Acland, MP, the chairman, remarked 'I don't suppose there has been a political meeting like this in the history of the Abbey Division.' The list of speakers included Sir Stafford Cripps, J B Priestley, Vernon Bartlett, and Geoffrey Mander.

particular policy might achieve for the country was brought down to earth with the simple question, 'And how is that going to benefit me?'

I did not experience the delights of polling day and the evening's knocking up. Obviously I had done more walking in the campaign than I should have done and, although I had concentrated upon canvassing, which I could do at my own pace and pack up if I felt the strain, I had been on my feet too long.

The result was that my damaged leg became swollen, one scar was inflamed and out oozed a small piece of my shattered tibia. For years, I kept this sequestrum as a souvenir, but it became lost in the mists of time. However, its surfacing presented me with some immediate problems. Back to hospital I had to go for tests to establish whether or not it was a portent of further trouble.

After various X-rays, the doctor was most reassuring. He told me, 'You have several pieces of shrapnel and other bits of bone floating about in your leg. But I should not worry about them if I were you. They will probably work their way out in a similar fashion to the one that has surfaced.'

With this encouraging news I limped back home and, a little later, back to work, to await the results of the election.

A Labour Government, the Atomic Bomb and Peace (Possibly!)

When the polls closed on 5 July, there could have been an awful anticlimax until the results were due to be announced three weeks later, but life in the summer of 1945 knew of no such thing. It seemed that the entire personnel of HM forces was home on leave and their loved ones were throwing parties to celebrate. Where all the food and drink came from remains a mystery, for food was rationed and alcoholic drinks in short supply. Most pubs were not opening until 8 p.m. and, if one had the temerity to ask for a whisky, one was laughed out of the door.

Every weekend saw a wedding, a homecoming, or both, but buying wedding presents had its difficulties. Most useful gift items were on 'dockets', unobtainable, or too expensive. But glassware was one of the gifts that was available and many a newly married couple found themselves with enough glasses to drink themselves silly, if only the liquor had been available to fill them.

During this hectic period, I was in a pub with a group of friends on leave when it was suggested that we place a joint accumulator bet. We were all to subscribe 5s. (25p) and share the winnings that were certain to result. I have never been a gambler, not because of any moral scruples, but from my lack of desire to study form and learn the jargon of the racing pundits. So I sat back and listened to our self-styled experts as they made the momentous decisions.

In those days, gambling had its difficulties for most working class people. There were no betting shops and few workers had an account with a registered bookmaker. Instead, there were the street bookies, who ran illegal businesses with the aid of what were called 'runners'. These people, sometimes of a dubious character, would place the bets with the bookmaker and collect any winnings. The gambling fraternity also faced the difficulty that the writing of betting slips was forbidden in public houses. Publicans, who were in danger of losing their licence if such practices took place, came down heavily upon any customers compiling their bets. Hence, our experts had a hard time not only deciding which horses would win, but in placing their findings on paper.

The final bet was a master of probabilities and many expressions that I did not understand. But the die was cast, the 5s. collected and the bet dispatched; all we had to do was to wait for the horses to do their stuff. Of course, somewhere in the maze of possibilities one of the nags was pipped at the post, with the result that a handsome win was reduced to our getting our money back and each individual gaining the huge sum of sixpence for all the effort involved. I was hardly lured into the temptations of gambling.

In July, the weather was pleasant and, for the first time in years, Londoners were able to visit the seaside resorts for a holiday. Most of the holiday camps were still occupied by the military, but there was much talk of grand re-openings for the next year.

On the international front, a high-powered conference opened in Potsdam (Germany) on 16 July. The issues before the conference were of major importance and the resulting communiqués could not conceal the rift that was widening between the Soviet Union and the Western Allies. In case he had been defeated at the election, Churchill invited Clement Attlee, the leader of the Labour Party, to attend as part of the British delegation to ensure the continuity of Britain's contribution.

Meanwhile, on my return to work after the recent problems with my leg, I had to go to a postal school to learn the art of primary sorting. When letters arrived from the pillar boxes and other collection points, they had to be divided into the main divisions for which the Post Office had a system of distribution. This meant that I had to learn 'Post Office geography', whereby the Midlands division stretched from Bedfordshire to Northumberland, whilst the North-West division covered most of England west of the Pennines. All places north of the border were designated 'Scotch'.

For three weeks I sat before a sorting frame with a huge pack of cards, which carried the names of different towns on their front and the correct sorting division on their back. I spent all day putting these cards into an array of pigeonholes, until I learnt which went where. When I had memorised one pack, my kindly supervisor provided me with another.

The Great Day Dawns!

Thursday, 26 July came and little attention was paid to the location of any town. Although there were no transistor radios, the news of the election gradually filtered through from the communal wireless set in the canteen. The number of Labour gains quickly mounted and became a landslide; Churchill had been swept from office. To my delight, two Communist MPs had been elected.

I had no adult memories of Labour Governments, for I was only a babe in arms when the first Labour Government took power in 1924 and seven years old when the second Labour administration had ended in the disaster of 1931. But I was well aware of the role of Ramsay MacDonald and the bitter reactions to what he had done. I was also aware that both of these Labour administrations were minority affairs and had to rely upon Liberal MPs for support. But now, for the first time ever, Labour had a decisive majority. How would it use it?

Various people then suggested to me that I should join the Labour Party. It was claimed that vital lessons had been learnt from the disasters of the 1930s and that they were unlikely to be repeated now that Labour had such a commanding Parliamentary position.

Obviously I could not foresee the terrible problems that faced the new government, but I was convinced that no Social Democratic administration could ever achieve Socialism. Was I not familiar with Lenin's *State and Revolution* which decreed that it was not only necessary to change governments but vital to change the whole apparatus of the state? Reforms were all very well, but at twenty-one years of age my money was on Communist ideas that had overthrown a repressive regime in Russia and whose government would have made giant steps towards Socialism but for the War. This simplistic analysis of the situation led me back into the ranks of the Young Communist League and forward into the Party itself.

All over the weekend that followed the results, there were celebrations in the party rooms and pubs. Clement Attlee was in residence at Number 10 and we awaited the naming of his cabinet. Within days, the Left received its first disappointment: Ernest Bevin had been appointed Foreign Secretary.

Bevin had been Minister of Labour in the Coalition Government and had done a brilliant job in organising the country's manpower during the War. But, apart from being an outstanding organiser, he was an arch-enemy of the Left. He was an extremely blunt and undiplomatic person; it was well known that he was daggers drawn with Herbert Morrison, Home Secretary during the War, and he had not spoken to Sir Walter Citrine, Secretary of the TUC, for years. At the Labour Party Conference of 1936, Bevin had demolished the well-respected veteran Labour leader, George Lansbury, in a savage personal attack. Even if blunt speaking were necessary in opposition to the Soviet Union, was Bevin, the man who could fall out with his colleagues, the right choice to lead negotiations with France, the United States, and other world powers?

Some on the Left suggested a 'Bevin must go' campaign, but the general opinion was to give Bevin a chance. In any case, the euphoria of the Labour victory was too great to let one appointment spoil the picture and, before serious work started, the August Bank holiday was upon us. In those days the holiday always fell on the first Monday in August and that year it was to be the 6th.

6 August and the Character of Warfare Changes

The record of weather on an August Bank Holiday is notorious for sending fresh air enthusiasts scuttling for cover as the rain pours down to spoil the last outdoor holiday of the year. But that of 1945 was an exception to the rule; the sun shone and it was ideal to spend a romantic day in the country. And so, on that fateful Bank Holiday Monday, my girlfriend and I set out to enjoy the delights of the area around Amersham that I had got to know so well just two years earlier. All was pleasant and peaceful, but on the other side of the globe a catastrophic event had occurred.

It was over tea on our return that we learnt that one single atomic bomb had been dropped by the Americans that had destroyed the Japanese town of Hiroshima, killed about one hundred and forty thousand people and injured countless more. The fact that one bomb could inflict such damage made the efforts of the RAF to raze the principal German cities to the ground over a period of some five years appear small beer. Obviously, the ramifications of this new weapon were enormous.

No time was lost before widespread discussions began and divisions of opinion emerged. One main school of thought was that Japan would now have to surrender immediately and that this would save many Allied lives as the costly invasion of Pacific islands and the mainland itself would prove unnecessary. On the other hand, there was the claim this was only a short-term appraisal of this weapon of mass destruction.

During the first weeks of August, before detailed assessments of the new bomb were made, I think it is fair to say that the majority of people seemed in favour of it being used. An early edition of the Communist *Daily Worker* argued that the bomb would shorten the War and that could only be good.

In modern times, Japan had been remarkably successful in its military affairs. It had defeated China in 1896, humbled Imperial Russia in 1905, been on the winning side of the Allies in the First World War, inflicted further defeats on China between 1931 and 1945, ruled the roost in the Far East in 1940–41 even before Pearl Harbour, and made spectacular gains against the Western powers in 1941–1945. As part of its military code, the idea of surrender was anathema. Therefore, despite the horrors of Hiroshima, the Japanese Government prevaricated about surrendering and so, three days later (the 9th) a second atomic bomb was dropped, this time on the city of Nagasaki. Although the second bomb was more powerful than the first, owing to the geological features of Nagasaki the death toll was less and only amounted to some ninety-five thousand people.[1]

When the Nagasaki bomb was dropped we wondered how much

---

[1] Gilbert, *Second World War*, 1999, Chapters 50–51.

longer the Japanese Government could hold out, and behind the scenes in Japan there was a fierce dispute between the military and political factions concerning whether or not the War was to continue. These divisions in Japan were reflected in the radio broadcast of the Japanese Emperor – who many thought should have faced trial as a war criminal – when he said on the day of surrender:

> 'Should we continue to fight, it would not only result in the collapse and obliteration of the Japanese nation but would lead to the total extinction of human civilisation.'

For once the Emperor had got it right.

Between the dropping of the two bombs, the Soviet Union declared war on Japan (8 August), exactly three months after the defeat of Germany and in accordance with the promise it had made at the Yalta conference in February 1945. I remember that this brought me into a heated argument with a work colleague, who accused the Russians of opportunism. The fact that the Russians did not know that the War was going to end much quicker than anticipated had to be spelt out, and I was not slow in stressing that, for three years, the Russians had borne the brunt of the fighting in Europe.

But Russia's declaration and subsequent actions were to have major consequences for Far Eastern affairs. Within days, Communist forces began to sweep down into Korea, stopping short at the 38th parallel, to meet the American forces that had swept up from the south of the country. Thus, the stage was set for a bloody localised war, which in 1950 nearly spilled over into an atomic international conflict.

With the end of hostilities, the British Government announced that victory over Japan would be celebrated on 15 and 16 of August (VJ Days) and so another round of festivities began. The state opening of Parliament coincided with the first of the two days and large, joyful crowds assembled outside Buckingham Palace. Prime Minister Attlee claimed, 'The last of our enemies is laid low.'

But I remember that this second round of celebrations was more muted than that of VE day. The sense of relief was not so great, as no Japanese bombs had fallen on London or any other British city. Then there was the suddenness of Japan's collapse.

Germany's defeat had been expected for several weeks and people had keyed themselves up accordingly, whereas, in the case of Japan, they were just not ready for the final curtain.

To add to the worries, it was now becoming clear that the wartime unity of the three main allies was starting to fragment and the future was becoming uncertain. The new President of the United States, Harry Truman, had adopted a much harder line against the Soviet Union, and he had also decreed that Lend-Lease, a means of vital economic aid that Britain had been deriving from the States, was to cease on VJ Day. The country was warned that it was facing an 'economic Dunkirk'.[2]

On top of this, many people were beginning to have second thoughts about the atomic bomb. Was it right to use such a weapon, when the main victims were women and children? What would be its effect upon the environment, and what might happen when other countries developed the weapon?

The fact that the defeat of the Axis powers had come in two stages had given time for reflection on the prospects for peace and dispelled some of the earlier euphoria. Yes, there were street parties, and many pubs ran out of beer, but the enormity of the difficulties of reconstruction was gradually emerging. One could readily agree with the VJ Day message of King George VI, when in a radio broadcast he said:

> ...there is not one of us who has experienced this terrible war who does not realise that we shall feel its inevitable consequences long after we have all forgotten our rejoicings today.

Indeed, his statement may be seen as a curtain raiser for the post-war years.

The Japanese representatives signed the formal surrender of their country to the American Supremo, General MacArthur, on 2 September and, at last, the War was officially over. Now the majority of servicemen were anxiously waiting for their demobilisation numbers to come up, so that they could get on with the rest of their lives.

---

[2] Taylor, *English History, 1914–1945*, 1965, Chapter 16.

Sixty Years On and Time to Reflect

The six-year period between the ages of fifteen and twenty-one is important in the mental and physical development of any individual. But I belong to a generation that was born to face the awful culling machinery of modern warfare. So what lessons did I learn and could I, given the restrictions on choice, have played things any differently?

If I turn to the Blitz of London when I was sixteen years of age, I feel that I sailed through this stormy period fairly easily, mainly because I was lucky, young, and did not appreciate the dangers involved. Had I been hurt, I am sure that it would have eaten into my ration of courage and influenced my future conduct.

When the main round of the Blitz finished in May 1941, the Germans did not announce that, for the immediate future, they would be concentrating their efforts in the east, and it was only slowly that life in London returned to something like normal. But it was not normal. There was the disappearance of colleagues and friends as the long arm of National Service reached out and whisked them away. This underlined the fact that one's turn would be coming soon.

Two things stand out in my memories of this period. The task of delivering telegrams carrying the news of loved ones killed in action was one that made me realise the awful heartbreaks that every conflict invokes. On a lighter note, despite all the wartime influences, I had a great social life in the eighteen-month period before I joined the army at the end of 1942. My membership of a youth club and the Young Communist League, plus the long hours I was working in the Post Office, gave me a full and creative week. There was just not enough time to fit everything in. Today when I see young people hanging around street corners, bored out of their mind, I wonder what has gone wrong.

The Army (as I knew it)

When I joined the army, I realised that it was a central feature of the Establishment. The monarch was at its head, and the Church of England (the Tory Party at prayer) in close support. It had served most of the country's imperial interests, and Colonel Blimp was still in evidence. I was well aware that I was not joining a Socialist organisation.

My memories of the army have their contradictions. In many ways I hated it, but, like the famous curate's egg, it was good in places, and I was aware that it was a necessary institution if fascism were to be defeated.

I cannot claim that my career in the army was successful; I joined as a private and rose to no other rank. My experiences were those of one who was at the bottom of the chain of command, enjoyed none of the privileges of the officers' mess, and had to do what I was told or face humiliating consequences. I have often wondered whether or not, if I had worked for and gained promotion, my attitude towards the army would be the same. But would I have survived to tell the tale?

It is obvious that no army can operate if there has to be a meeting of a joint shop stewards committee before any action can be undertaken. On the other hand, does it make sense that all orders must be obeyed immediately, even if it is clear that their execution will result in disaster? Does not Nelson's 'blind eye' episode illustrate the weakness of the complete obedience concept? So where should the line be drawn between the two extremes?

I had no idea then and I have no idea now. One may note that the Greek philosopher Plato, some 2400 years ago, had to wrestle with the problems of reconciling the principles of democracy with strong leadership, and the debate continues today.

Then there was, and probably still is, the nonsense that the army teaches a young man discipline. This has always struck me as doublespeak for 'if you don't do what you are told, we'll knock the shit out of you'. I have long believed that the only form of worthwhile discipline is self-discipline and this played but a small role in the army's teachings.

A common expression in my time was, 'Bullshit baffles

brains'. One could see the truth in this saying when one realised that the many hours spent on Blancoing and polishing awkward pieces of brass on one's equipment are all wasted when, at the onset of any battle, all brasses are dulled and faces dirtied. Yes, I joined in the frantic Friday evening preparations for a barrack-room inspection the next day, when every conceivable object was either scrubbed or polished. I had no choice. But I could not help thinking that the exercise was merely a ploy for keeping the lower ranks in their place. Otherwise, why was it necessary, for example, for fuel bin lids to shine like a mirror, and brooms to be cleaned so that they looked as if the last thing they had been used for was to sweep the floor?

Part of the bullshit scenario was 'square-bashing' (parade-ground drill). Hours were wasted marching up and down, keeping in step, shouldering and ordering arms, and all for what? Was the enemy likely to surrender when he saw us advancing in perfect formation, or more likely to pick up his Spandau machine-gun and mow the lot of us down in rapid succession? When I think of how successful the guerrilla armies were when they operated with iron discipline in matters deemed essential, but none in what was considered trivia, it makes me wonder why we wasted time on activities and practices that were more suited to a peacetime army.

My last thoughts on the army concern compulsory church parades. On a Sunday morning when such a parade had been ordered there was more swearing and blaspheming than the rest of the week. The idea of going on parade to be shouted at, then marching off to hear a sermon about loving one's fellow man when the art of killing had been the order of the week, was impossible to reconcile, at least for me.

The Communist Party

Had I been a little older and wiser when I joined the army, I would not have tried to convert it into a Red army. I learnt later in my political life that there are times to press a case and times to keep quiet. Nevertheless, I do not regret speaking out at the organised current affairs discussions on the iniquities of the economic system that had caused so much misery in the 1930s, the period in which we had all grown up. Nor do I regret continuing my arguments in the barrack room at night. It has been said that the army's discussion groups helped to ensure the huge servicemen's vote for Labour in the General Election of 1945, and I am pleased that I played my part.

A key subject in any Communist's arguments was to advocate the immediate opening of a Second Front. Many on the Left thought that the delay was due to a political desire for Germany and the Soviet Union to destroy each other after, so that the Western powers could dominate Europe. Now, many years later and having read many of the accounts of the Normandy fighting, I feel that any invasion attempt made much before June 1944 would have ended in disaster. There are many issues involved in this matter and no doubt they will be discussed for many years to come.

Final Thoughts

The cost of the War in lives, money and misery is inestimable. Nevertheless, despite all that had to be endured, I am glad that my generation contributed to the defeat of Nazi Germany and the other Axis powers. On this issue I have no second thoughts whatever.

There is one other way in which my wartime experiences have influenced my everyday life. Like all human beings, there are times when I get fed up or discontented over some issue or other. On such occasions, I think of my former comrades who, for the last sixty years, have been occupying a grave in Normandy. They would, I am sure, be only too happy to be alive and face the niggling matters bugging me. Then, any problem that I may have seems completely unimportant.

Printed in the United Kingdom
by Lightning Source UK Ltd.
120384UK00001B/19-57